I0425994

DEPARTMENT OF THE NAVY
Headquarters United States Marine Corps
Washington, D.C. 20308-1775

24 September 2002

FOREWORD

As Marines serving on joint or staff billets, we are frequently called upon to provide the Marine Corps perspective on current issues, to discuss the roles and missions of the Corps, or to explain how Marines prepare and equip to fight. Much of this information is published in joint and Service doctrine. Marine Corps Reference Publication (MCRP) 5-1A, *Doctrinal References for Expeditionary Maneuver Warfare*, is a compendium of current joint and Service doctrinal publications. The intent of this publication is to provide Marine officers and staff noncommissioned officers with a quick reference guide to the essential elements of published information that they need to effectively serve on component, joint, or multinational staffs. MCRP 5-1A is not inclusive, and staff officers should refer to higher level doctrine as needed.

Reviewed and approved this date.

BY DIRECTION OF THE COMMANDANT OF THE MARINE CORPS

EDWARD HANLON, JR.
Lieutenant General, U.S. Marine Corps
Commanding General
Marine Corps Combat Development Command

Publication Control Number: 144 000112 00

Table of Contents

Operational Environment
• • • • • • •

The environment where Marines will operate in the next decade reflects the changing character of modern conflict. The growth of cities along the world's littorals means Marines must be prepared to conduct a range of operations in heavily populated urban areas and that civilians and other noncombatants will be an ever-increasing concern to the commander. (Marine Corps Doctrinal Publication [MCDP] 1-0, *Marine Corps Operations*)

Levels of War

The highest level is the strategic. Strategy involves establishing goals, assigning forces, providing assets, and imposing conditions on the use of force. Strategy derives from political and policy objectives and is the sole authoritative basis for military operations. The strategic level of war involves the art of winning wars and maintaining the peace.

The next level—operational—links the strategic and tactical levels. It includes deciding when, where, and under what conditions to engage the enemy in battle. The operational level of war is the art and science of winning campaigns.

The final level of war is the tactical. Tactics are the concepts and methods used to accomplish a particular mission in either combat or military operations other than war (MOOTW). In war, tactics focus on applying combat power to defeat an enemy force. The tactical level of war involves the art and science of winning engagements and battles to achieve the objectives of the campaign.

The distinctions between the levels of war are rarely clear and often overlap in practice. Commanders may operate at multiple levels simultaneously. In MOOTW, small unit leaders may conduct tactical actions that have operational and even strategic consequences.

Range of Military Operations

Conflict can take a variety of forms ranging from general war, such as a global conflict between major powers, all the way down to MOOTW where violence is limited and combat forces may not be needed. This range may be characterized by two major categories: a major theater war (MTW) or a smaller-scale contingency.

An MTW is the employment of large joint and multinational forces in combat operations to defeat an enemy nation, coalition, or alliance. Operation Desert Storm is an example of an MTW.

A smaller-scale contingency normally encompasses a wide range of naval, joint, or multinational operations in small wars and MOOTW. Peace enforcement operations in the Balkans and foreign humanitarian assistance operations are examples of smaller-scale contingencies.

Unified Action
● ● ● ● ● ● ●

Unified action is a generic term that refers to a broad scope of activities (including the synchronization of activities with governmental and nongovernmental agencies) taking place within unified commands, subunified commands, or joint task forces under the overall direction of the commanders of those commands. The national military strategy calls for the Marine Corps to act as part of fully interoperable and integrated joint forces. The joint force commander (JFC) synchronizes the employment of Marine Corps forces with that of the other Services to fully exploit the capabilities of the joint force and to effectively and efficiently accomplish the mission. (MCDP 1-0)

Joint Operations

Joint operations are operations that include forces of two or more Military Departments under a single commander. Joint force commanders use joint forces within their area of operations (AOs) to participate in engagement activities and to conduct military operations in support of the geographic combatant commanders' contingency and war plans. Combatant commanders and their staffs are responsible for preparing plans for engagement with other nations and their forces throughout the theater. They also must prepare and maintain contingency and war plans for their theater of operations.

Multinational Operations, Alliances, and Coalitions

Although the United States may act unilaterally when the situation requires, it pursues its national interests through alliances and coalitions when possible. Alliances and coalitions can provide larger and more capable forces, share the costs of the operation, and enhance the legitimacy of the operation in world and United States (US) public opinion. Multinational operations are usually conducted within the structure of an alliance or coalition. Alliances normally have established agreements for long-term objectives, developed contingency plans, and standardized some equipment and procedures to ease interoperability. Coalitions are normally established for shorter periods or for specific multinational operations. They normally do not have established procedures or standardized equipment. Unity of command is difficult to achieve in multinational operations. To compensate for this, commanders concentrate on obtaining unity of effort among the participating national forces. Consensus building is the key element in building unity of effort in multinational operations.

Roles, Missions, and Functions

Roles are the broad and enduring purposes for which the Services and US Special Operations Command (USSOCOM) were established by Congress. Missions are the tasks assigned by the President or Secretary of Defense to the combatant commanders. Functions are specific responsibilities assigned by the President and Secretary of Defense to enable the Services to fulfill their legally established roles. Various laws, directives, and manuals establish the roles and functions of the Marine Corps and describe the general composition and responsibilities of the Marine Corps. The key sources are Title 10, United States Code: *Armed Forces*; *Goldwater-Nichols Department of Defense Reorganization Act of 1986*; Department of Defense Directive 5100.1, *Functions of the Department of Defense and Its Major Components*; and the *Marine Corps Manual*. (MCDP 1-0)

Title 10, United States Code: *Armed Forces*

Chapter 507, Section 5063 details the Marine Corps' composition and functions. The Marine Corps—

- Shall be organized to include not less than three combat divisions and three aircraft wings, and other organic land combat forces, aviation, and services.

- Shall be organized, trained, and equipped to provide Fleet Marine Forces of combined arms, together with supporting aviation forces, for service with the fleet in the seizure and defense of advanced naval bases and for the conduct of such land operations as may be essential to the prosecution of a naval campaign.

- Shall provide detachments and organizations for service on armed vessels of the Navy, shall provide security detachments for the protection of naval property at naval stations and bases, and shall perform such other duties as the President may direct. These additional duties may not detract from or interfere with the operations for which the Marine Corps is primarily organized.

- Shall develop, in coordination with the Army and Air Force, those phases of amphibious operations that pertain to the tactics, techniques, and equipment used by landing forces (LFs).

- Is responsible, in accordance with integrated joint mobilization plans, for the expansion of the peacetime components of the Marine Corps to meet the needs of war.

Goldwater-Nichols Department of Defense Reorganization Act of 1986

Salient features of the act are the—

- Service chiefs (Chief of Staff of the Army, Chief of Naval Operations, Chief of Staff of the Air Force, and Commandant of the Marine Corps) are responsible for organizing, training, and equipping Service forces, while combatant commanders are responsible for planning and executing joint operations.

- Chairman of the Joint Chiefs of Staff is the principal military advisor to the President, National Security Council, and the Secretary of Defense. The Chairman outranks all other officers of the Armed Forces, but does not exercise military command over the combatant commanders, Joint Chiefs of Staff, or any of the Armed Forces.

- Joint Staff is under the exclusive direction of the Chairman of the Joint Chiefs of Staff. It is organized along conventional staff lines to support the Chairman and the other members of the Joint Chiefs of Staff in performing their duties. The Joint Staff does not function as an overall Armed Forces General Staff and has no executive authority.

- Operational chain of command is clearly established from the President through the Secretary of Defense to the combatant commanders.

Department of Defense Directive 5100.1, *Functions of the Department of Defense and Its Major Components*

This directive defines the primary functions of the Marine Corps. Among these primary functions are to—

- Organize, train, equip, and provide Marine Corps forces to conduct prompt and sustained combat operations at sea, including seabased and land-based aviation. These forces will seek out and destroy enemy naval forces, suppress enemy sea commerce, gain and maintain general naval supremacy, control vital sea areas, protect vital sea lines of communications, establish and maintain local superiority in an area of naval operations, seize and defend advanced naval bases, and conduct land, air, and space operations essential to a naval campaign.

- Provide Marine Corps forces of combined arms for service with the Navy to seize and defend advanced naval bases and to conduct land operations necessary for a naval campaign. In addition, the Marine Corps shall provide detachments and organizations for service on armed vessels of the Navy and provide security detachments for naval stations and bases.

- Organize, equip, and provide Marine Corps forces to conduct joint amphibious operations. The Marine Corps is responsible for the amphibious training of all forces assigned to joint amphibious operations.

- Organize, train, equip, and provide forces for reconnaissance, antisubmarine warfare, protection of shipping, aerial refueling, and mine laying operations.

- Organize, train, equip, and provide forces for air and missile defense and space control operations.

- Provide equipment, forces, procedures, and doctrine to conduct and support electronic warfare.

- Organize, train, equip, and provide forces to conduct and support special operations.

- Organize, train, equip, and provide forces to conduct and support psychological operations.

Functions to be accomplished together with other Services include develop—

- The doctrine, procedures, and equipment of naval forces for amphibious operations and the doctrine and procedures for joint amphibious operations.

- The doctrine, tactics, techniques, and equipment employed by landing forces in amphibious operations. The Marine Corps has primary responsibility for the development of LF doctrine, tactics, techniques, and equipment that are of common interest to the Army and the Marine Corps.

- Doctrine, procedures, and equipment of interest to the Marine Corps for airborne operations not provided for by the Army.

- Doctrine, procedures, and equipment employed by Marine Corps forces in the conduct of space operations.

In addition to the above functions, the Marine Corps will perform such other duties as the President or the Secretary of Defense may direct. However, these additional duties must not detract from or interfere with the operations for which the Marine Corps is primarily organized. These functions do not contemplate the creation of a second land army. Finally, the directive describes collateral functions of the Marine Corps to train its forces to—

• Interdict enemy land and air forces and communications through operations at sea.

• Conduct close air and naval support for land operations.

• Furnish aerial photography for cartographic purposes.

• Participate in the overall air effort, when directed.

• Establish military government, as directed, pending transfer of this responsibility to other authority.

Marine Corps Manual

The *Marine Corps Manual* adds three more functions. The Marine Corps shall—

• Maintain a Marine Corps Forces Reserve (MARFORRES) for the purpose of providing trained units and qualified individuals to be available for active duty in the Marine Corps in time of war or national emergency and at such other times as the national security may require.

• Provide Marine Corps officer and enlisted personnel in support of the Department of State security program overseas.

• Organize Marine Corps aviation, as a collateral function, to participate as an integral component of naval aviation in the execution of such other Navy functions as the fleet commanders may direct.

Organization and Structure

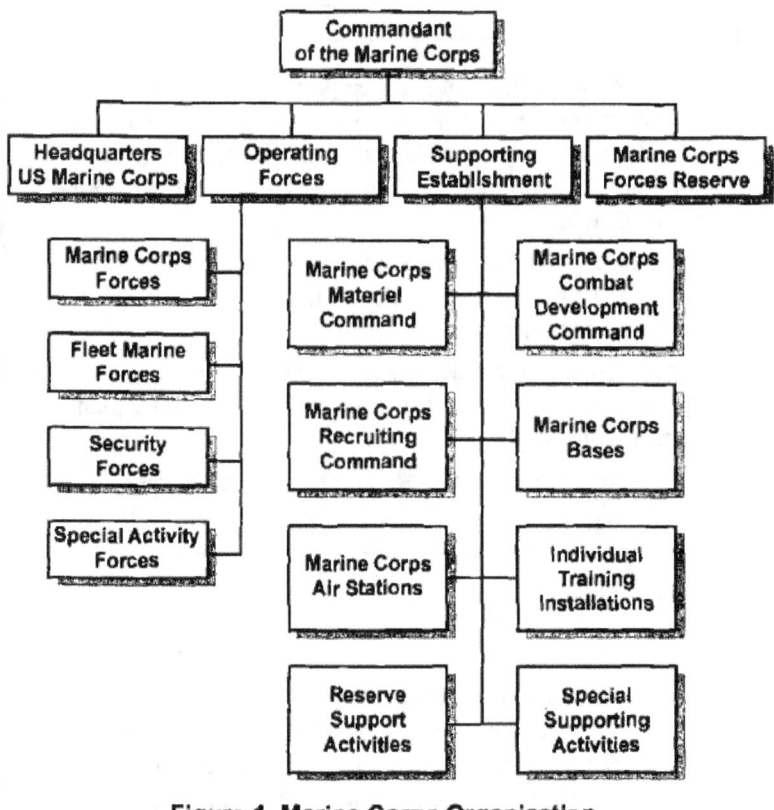

Figure 1. Marine Corps Organization.

As depicted in figure 1 on page 11, the Marine Corps' organization consists of Headquarters, US Marine Corps; the operating forces; the supporting establishment; and the MARFORRES. (MCDP 1-0)

Headquarters, US Marine Corps

The Commandant presides over the daily activities of Headquarters, US Marine Corps. Headquarters, US Marine Corps provides staff assistance to the Commandant by—

* Preparing the Marine Corps for employment. This is accomplished through recruiting, organizing, supplying, equipping (including research and development), training, servicing, mobilizing, demobilizing, administering, and maintaining the Marine Corps.

* Investigating and reporting on the efficiency of the Marine Corps and its preparation to support military operations by combatant commanders.

* Preparing detailed instructions for the execution of approved plans and supervising the execution of those plans and instructions.

* Coordinating the actions of organizations of the Marine Corps.

* Performing such other duties, not otherwise assigned by law, as may be prescribed by the Secretary of the Navy or the Commandant.

Operating Forces

Assigned Marine Corps Forces

All Marine Corps combat, combat support, and combat service support units are part of the assigned Marine Corps forces. Normally, these forces are task-organized for employment as Marine air-ground task forces (MAGTFs).

The "Forces for Unified Commands" memorandum assigns Marine Corps operating forces to each of the combatant commands. Although there are five Marine Corps components, there are only two Marine Corps component commands. The Marine Corps has established two combatant command-level Service component commands: Marine Corps Forces, Atlantic (MARFORLANT), and Marine Corps Forces, Pacific (MARFORPAC). The II Marine Expeditionary Force (II MEF) is provided by Commander, Marine Corps Forces, Atlantic (COMMARFORLANT), to the Commander, US Joint Forces Command, and the I and III MEFs are provided by Commander, Marine Corps Forces, Pacific (COMMARFORPAC), to the Commander, US Pacific Command.

The COMMARFORLANT, is assigned to the Commander, US Joint Forces Command, and the COMMARFORPAC, is assigned to the Commander, US Pacific Command. In order to provide three-star, general officer representation to the remaining three geographic combatant commands, COMMARFORLANT, is designated as the Marine Corps component commander to both Commander, US European Command, and Commander, US Southern Command. The COMMARFORPAC, is designated as the Marine Corps component commander to the Commander, US Central Command.

In addition to Service component responsibilities for US Pacific Command and US Central Command, COMMARFORPAC has multiple responsibilities in Korea. COMMARFORPAC exercises Service component responsibilities over Marine Corps forces as Commander, US Marine Corps Forces-Korea, and also exercises functional component responsibilities as Commander, Combined Marine Forces Command. These assignments reflect the peacetime disposition of Marine Corps forces. MEFs are apportioned to the geographic combatant commanders for contingency planning and are provided to these combatant commands when directed by the Secretary of Defense.

Assigned Marine Corps forces are commanded by a combatant command-level Marine Corps component commander. He is responsible for—

- Training and preparing Marine Corps forces for operational commitment commensurate with the strategic situation and the combatant commander's requirements.

- Advising the combatant commander on the proper employment of Marine Corps forces, participating in associated planning, and accomplishing such operational missions as may be assigned.

- Providing Service administration, discipline, intelligence, and operational support for assigned forces.

- Identifying requirements for support from the Marine Corps supporting establishment.

- Performing such other duties as may be directed.

Fleet Marine Forces
Fleet Marine Forces units serve with Navy fleets in the seizure or defense of advanced naval bases and in the conduct of such land operations as may be essential to the prosecution of naval operations in support of the joint campaign. When assigned, Fleet Marine Force units are commanded by the Commanding Generals, Fleet Marine Force, Atlantic, Europe, South, or Pacific. When the combatant commander tasks the Marine Corps component commander to provide assigned Marine Corps forces to the Navy component commander, the combatant command-level Marine Corps component commander CHOPs (change of operational control) MAGTFs and designated forces from Marine

Corps forces to the Navy component commander. These Fleet Marine Forces then serve with a numbered fleet or for naval operations and other commitments; e.g., deployed Marine expeditionary units (MEUs).

The relationship between Marine Corps forces and the Fleet Marine Force reflects the roles and functions of the Marine Corps. The Marine Corps has separate responsibilities to provide forces for use by the combatant commanders (Marine Corps forces) and by Navy operational commanders (Fleet Marine Forces) (see fig. 2).

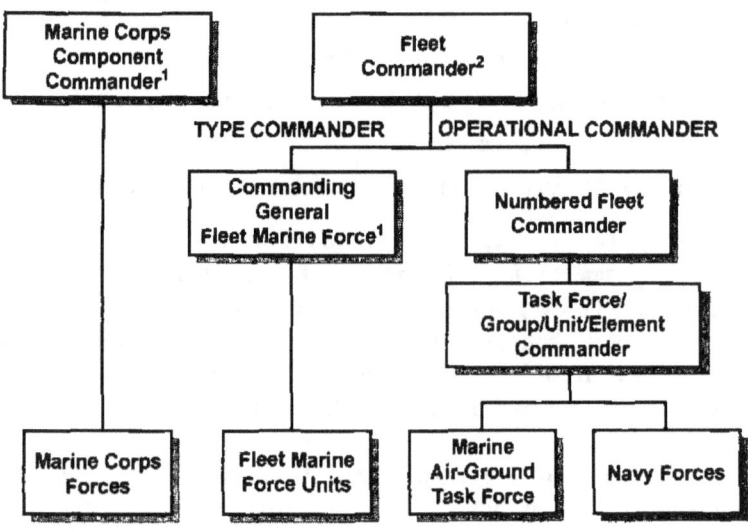

[1]The commanding general Fleet Marine Force is also the Marine Corps component commander.
[2]The fleet commander also has command responsibilities as the Navy component commander to the combatant commander.

Figure 2. Marine Corps Forces and Fleet Marine Relationships.

Security Forces

The 4th Marine Expeditionary Brigade (MEB) (Antiterrorism (AT)) provides the unified combatant commanders with a rapidly deployable and sustainable specialized antiterrorism force to deter, detect, and defend against terrorist actions and conduct initial incident response to combat the threat of terrorism worldwide. The 4th MEB (AT) provides the following capabilities:

- Chemical, biological, radiological, nuclear, and high explosive incident response.
- Physical and electronic security.
- Integrated vulnerability assessment and threat analysis.
- Explosive ordnance detection and disposal.
- Lethal and nonlethal weapons employment and training.
- Urban search and rescue.
- Physical security and antiterrorism/force protection training.

The 4th MEB (AT) deploys a forward command element (CE)/assessment team within 6 hours of notification and maintains a task-organized antiterrorism/incident response MAGTF on 12-hour alert. The entire MEB (AT) can deploy within 72 hours of notification. It may include an air contingency battalion/antiterrorism battalion, a Chemical/Biological Incident Response Force, Marine Corps Security Force Battalion elements, and Marine Security Guard Battalion elements. The Marine Corps Security Force Battalion provides armed antiterrorism and physical security trained forces to designated naval installations, vessels or units. The Battalion's Fleet Antiterrorism Security Team (FAST) companies provide Fleet combatant commanders and Fleet commanders forward-deployed FAST platoons for responsive short-term security augmentation of installations, ships or vital naval and national assets when force protection conditions have been elevated beyond the capabilities of the permanent security forces. Marine Corps Security Force Battalion companies operate under operational control (OPCON) of the designated Navy commanding officer and under the administrative control (ADCON) of the Commandant of the Marine Corps through the Commanding General, Fleet Marine Force, Atlantic.

Special Activity Forces

Special activity forces provide security or services or perform other certain special type duties for agencies other than the Department of the Navy. Assignment of personnel to and the mission of these forces are specified by the supported agency and approved by the Commandant. The Marine Corps provides Marines from the Marine Security Guard Battalion to meet the security guard detachment requirements at foreign service posts throughout the world. The Marine Security Guard detachment mission is to provide internal security services to selected Department of State embassies, consulates, and legations to prevent the compromise of classified material and equipment and protect United States citizens and government property. Marine Security Guard detachments operate under the OPCON of the Secretary of State and under the ADCON of the Commandant of the Marine Corps via the Commander, Marine Corps Forces, Atlantic/Commanding General 4th MEB (AT).

The Marine Air-Ground Task Force

The MAGTF is a balanced, air-ground combined arms task organization of Marine Corps forces under a single commander, structured to accomplish a specific mission. It is the Marine Corps' principal organization for all missions across the range of military operations. It is designed to fight, while having the ability to prevent conflicts and control crises. All MAGTFs are task-organized and vary in size and capability according to the assigned mission, threat, and battlespace environment. They are specifically tailored for rapid deployment by air or sea and ideally suited for a forward presence role. (MCDP 1-0)

Elements

All MAGTFs are expeditionary by design and comprised of four core elements: a command element (CE), a ground combat element (GCE), an aviation combat element (ACE), and a combat service support element (CSSE). See figure 3.

The MAGTF's combat forces reside within these four elements. Although MAGTFs will differ because of mission and forces assigned, a standard procedure exists for organization, planning, and operations. As a modular organization, the MAGTF is tailorable to each mission through task organization. This building block approach also makes reorganization a matter of routine. In addition to the Marine Corps units, MAGTFs may have attached forces from other Services and nations; e.g., naval

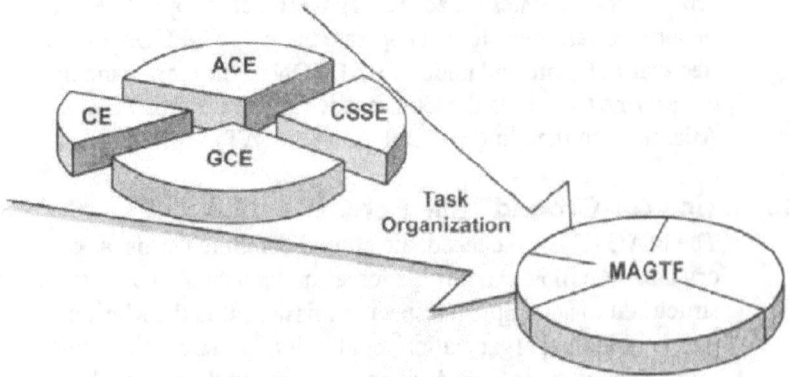

Figure 3. MAGTF Organization.

construction force, multiple launch rocket system batteries, and armor brigades. A key feature of Marine expeditionary organization is expandability. Crisis response requires the ability to expand the expeditionary force after its introduction into the theater without sacrificing the continuity of operational capability. The MAGTF's modular structure lends itself to rapid expansion into a larger force as a situation demands by adding forces, as needed, to the core units of each existing element. This expandability includes expanding into a joint or multinational force because the MAGTF structure parallels the structure of a multidimensional joint force. Operation Restore Hope in Somalia is an example of the MAGTF's expandability. This contingency began with the employment of a MEU (special operations capable) (MEU[SOC]) to seize the port and airport in Mogadishu, enabling the deployment of elements of I MEF via air and maritime prepositioning ships (MPS), with the MEF eventually employing a brigade-sized force to provide security and humanitarian relief to the Somalis. On missions where Marine forces are not deployed as part of a MAGTF (such as the Chemical/ Biological Incident Response Force), Marine security forces, or forces assigned to battle forest fires, the Marine Corps component commander plays an increasingly important role in ensuring the Marine forces are properly equipped, trained, and employed. Marine forces deployed as a MAGTF are normally employed by the JFC as a MAGTF. As a task-organized force, the MAGTF's size and composition depend on the committed mission. If a MAGTF is deprived of a part of its combat forces, accomplishment of the mission for which it is tailored is jeopardized. However, on a day-to-day basis, the MAGTF may be tasked to conduct operations in support of another force and will identify capabilities (e.g., air sorties, beach and port operations, and civil affairs) excess to its mission requirements to the JFC that may be of use to other components of the joint force.

Command Element. The CE is the MAGTF headquarters. As with all other MAGTF elements, it is task-organized to provide the command and control capabilities necessary for effective planning, execution, and assessment of operations across the warfighting functions. Additionally, the CE can exercise command and control within a joint force from the sea or ashore and act as a core element around which a joint task force headquarters may be formed, provide interagency coordination for MOOTW, and conduct "reach back." The six warfighting functions are command and control, maneuver, fires, intelligence, logistics, and force protection. A CE may include additional command and control and intelligence capabilities from national assets and theater, force reconnaissance company assets, signals intelligence capabilities from the radio battalion, and a force fires coordination center. A CE can employ additional major subordinate commands such as the force field artillery headquarters, naval construction regiments, or Army maneuver or engineering units.

Ground Combat Element. The GCE is task-organized to conduct ground operations, project combat power, and contribute to battlespace dominance in support of the MAGTF's mission. It is formed around an infantry organization reinforced with artillery, reconnaissance, assault amphibian, tank, and engineer forces. The GCE can vary in size and composition from a rifle platoon to one or more Marine divisions. It is the only element that can seize and occupy terrain.

Aviation Combat Element. The ACE is task-organized to conduct air operations, project combat power, and contribute to battlespace dominance in support of the MAGTF's mission by performing some or all of the six functions of Marine aviation: antiair warfare, offensive air support, assault support, electronic warfare, air reconnaissance, and control of aircraft and missiles.

It is formed around an aviation headquarters with air control agencies, aircraft squadrons or groups, and combat service support units. It can vary in size and composition from an aviation detachment of specifically required aircraft to one or more Marine aircraft wings. The ACE may be employed from ships or forward expeditionary land bases and can readily transition between seabases and land bases without loss of capability. It has the capability of conducting command and control across the battlespace.

Combat Service Support Element. The CSSE is task-organized to provide all functions of tactical logistics necessary to support the continued readiness and sustainability of the MAGTF. The six functions of tactical logistics are supply, maintenance, transportation, health services, engineering, and other services, which include legal, exchange, food, disbursing, postal, billeting, religious, mortuary, and morale and recreation services. See MCDP 4, *Logistics*, for a detailed discussion. The CSSE is formed around a combat service support headquarters and may vary in size and composition from a support detachment to one or more force service support groups. The CSSE, operating from seabases or from expeditionary bases established ashore, enables sustainment of forces, thus extending MAGTF's capabilities in time and space. It may be the main effort of the MAGTF during foreign humanitarian assistance missions or selected phases of maritime prepositioning force (MPF) operations.

Supporting Establishment. The supporting establishment is often referred to as the "fifth element of the MAGTF." It is vital to the success of Marine Corps forces conducting expeditionary operations. It recruits, trains, equips, and sustains Marines, enabling them to conduct expeditionary operations in increasingly complex and dangerous environments. Bases and stations of the supporting establishment provide the training areas, ranges, and the modeling and simulation facilities necessary to prepare Marines and their units for combat. These posts of the Corps serve as staging and marshalling areas for deploying units and often are the continental United States (CONUS) end of a responsive replacement, supply, and new equipment pipeline into the AO. The Marines, Sailors, and civilians of the supporting establishment are true partners with the Marines of the operating forces in accomplishing the mission. Bases and stations of the supporting establishment also provide facilities and support to the families of deployed Marines, allowing Marines to concentrate fully on their demanding missions without undue concern for the welfare of their families.

Types

MAGTFs are integrated combined arms forces structured to accomplish specific missions. MAGTFs are generally categorized in the following four types.

Marine Expeditionary Force. The MEF is the Marine Corps' principal warfighting organization. It can conduct and sustain expeditionary operations in any geographic environment. MEFs are the sole standing MAGTFs; i.e., they exist in peacetime as well as wartime. Size and composition can vary greatly, depending on the requirements of the mission. A MEF is normally commanded by a lieutenant general.

Marine Expeditionary Brigade. The MEB is the "middle-weight" MAGTF. It is a crisis response force capable of forcible entry and enabling the introduction of follow-on forces. It can serve as part of a joint or multinational force and can provide the nucleus of a joint task force headquarters. It is unique in that it is the smallest MAGTF with a fully capable aviation element that performs all six functions of Marine aviation and is self-sustaining for 30 days. A MEB is capable of rapid deployment and employment deploying either by air, in combination with the MPS, or by amphibious shipping. Currently, the 1st, 2d, and 3d MEBs have been designated within I, II, and III MEF and are commanded by the deputy MEF commanders or other general officers.

Marine Expeditionary Unit (Special Operations Capable). The MEU(SOC) is the standard forward-deployed Marine expeditionary organization. A forward-deployed MEU(SOC) provides an immediate seabased response to meet forward presence and power projection requirements. A MEU(SOC) is commanded by a colonel and deploys with 15 days of supplies.

Special Purpose MAGTF. A special purpose MAGTF is a nonstanding MAGTF temporarily formed to conduct a specific mission for which a MEF or other unit is either inappropriate or unavailable. They are organized, trained, and equipped to conduct such a mission. Special purpose MAGTFs have been deployed for a wide variety of missions, such as humanitarian relief and coalition training. Designation of a special purpose MAGTF is based on the mission it is assigned ("Special Purpose MAGTF Hurricane Relief"), the location in which it will operate ("Special Purpose MAGTF Somalia") or the name of the exercise in which it will participate ("Special Purpose MAGTF Unitas"). An important type of special purpose MAGTF is the air contingency force (ACF). An ACF is an on-call, task-organized alert force that is maintained by all three MEFs. An ACF can deploy within 18 hours of notification. It can be dispatched virtually worldwide to respond to a rapidly developing crisis. The ACF is the MEF's force in readiness. It can deploy independently or in conjunction with amphibious forces, MPFs, or other expeditionary forces. Because it can deploy so rapidly, readiness is paramount. Equipment and supplies intended for use as part of an ACF are identified and, where appropriate, stored and staged for immediate deployment. Personnel continuously focus on their tactical readiness. The ACF is airlifted to a secure airfield and carries its own initial sustainment.

Supporting Establishment

The supporting establishment assists in the training, sustainment, equipping, and embarkation of deploying forces. The supporting establishment includes—

- Marine Corps Materiel Command.
- Marine Corps Combat Development Command.
- Marine Corps Recruiting Command.
- Marine Corps bases.
- Marine Corps air stations.
- Individual training installations.
- Reserve support activities.
- Special supporting activities.

Marine Corps Forces Reserve

Marine Corps Forces Reserve is an integral part of Marine Corps Total Force. It is organized, trained, and equipped under the direction of the Commandant and commanded by the Commander, Marine Corps Forces Reserve (COMMARFORRES). The COMMARFORRES provides trained and qualified units and individuals to be available for active duty in time of war, national emergency, and at such other times as the national security may require. In recent years, the MARFORRES has been increasingly called upon to provide peacetime operational support. This operational support enhances the entire Marine Corps' operational readiness and reduces the strain of the operational tempo on the Active forces. The MARFORRES also maintains close contact with the American public through community outreach and operates Reserve training centers that ensure forces are ready in the event of mobilization. Like the Active forces, it is a combined arms force with balanced ground, aviation, and combat service support units. The MARFORRES includes a division, wing, and force service support group and unique capabilities such as civil affairs groups, aviation aggressor squadrons, and air-naval gunfire liaison companies. Reserve units routinely exercise with the Active forces and are assigned operational responsibilities. MARFORRES units and individuals are available for employ- ment on short notice after mobilization and any required refresher training. They can provide augmentation, reinforcement or recon- stitution of regular Marine Corps forces to satisfy mission requirements. The MARFORRES shares the same commitment to expeditionary readiness as the active duty Marine Corps.

Joint Operations Conducted through Service Component Commanders

A JFC may conduct operations through the Service component commanders. Conducting operations through Service compo- nents has certain advantages, including clear and uncomplicated command lines. This relationship is appropriate when stability, continuity, economy, ease of long-range planning, and scope of operations dictate preserving the organizational integrity of Service forces. These conditions apply when most of the required functions in a particular dimension are unique to a single-Service force or when Service force capabilities or responsibilities do not significantly overlap. In addition, Service component commands provide administrative and logistic support for their forces in a joint operation.

When the JFC conducts joint operations through Service component commanders, the Marine Corps component commander and the other Service component commanders have command—OPCON and ADCON—of their assigned Service forces. The JFC may also establish a support relationship between Service components to facilitate operations. Support is a command authority. A superior commander establishes a support relationship between subordinate commanders when one should aid, protect, complement, or sustain the other. The four categories of support are general, mutual, direct, and close. See MCDP 1-0.1, *Componency*.

Joint Operations Conducted through Functional Component Commanders

A JFC may conduct operations through functional components or employ them primarily to coordinate selected functions. Regardless of how the JFC organizes the assigned or attached forces, a Marine Corps component is included to provide administrative and logistic support for the assigned or attached Marine Corps forces (see fig. 4).

Functional components may be established across the range of military operations to perform operational missions that may be of short or extended duration. Functional components can be appropriate when forces from two or more Military Departments must operate in the same dimension or medium or there is a need to accomplish a distinct aspect of the assigned mission. *Functional components are components of a joint force and do not constitute a "joint force" with the authorities and responsibilities of a joint force.*

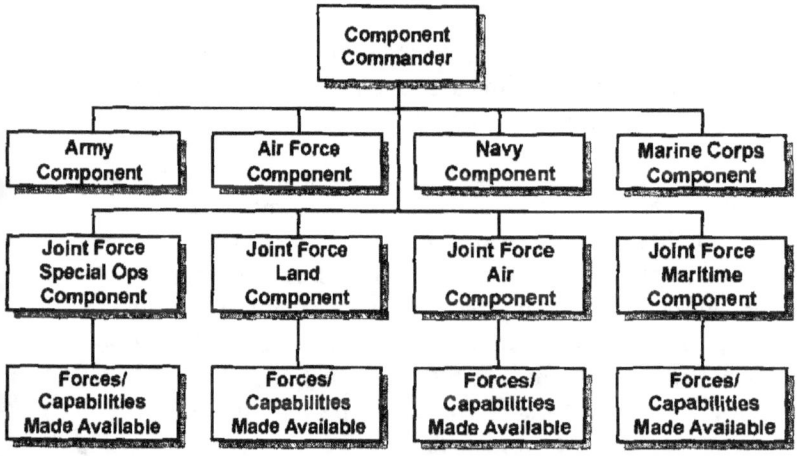

**Figure 4. Combatant Command
Organized by Functional Components.**

When the JFC centralizes direction and control of certain functions or types of joint operations under functional component commanders, the command relationships must be established. The JFC must designate the military capability that will be made available for tasking by the functional component commander and the appropriate command relationship(s) the functional component commander will exercise. For example, a joint force special operations component commander normally has OPCON of assigned forces and a joint force air component commander is normally delegated tactical control (TACON) of air defense, long-range interdiction, or long-range reconnaissance sorties or other military capability made available. The policy for the command and control of Marine Corps aviation, specifically covered by the Chairman of the Joint Chiefs of Staff "Policy for

Command and Control of USMC Tactical Air in Sustained Operations Ashore," is found in Joint Publication (JP) 0-2, *Unified Action Armed Forces (UNAAF)*.

The Marine Corps component commander retains command—OPCON and ADCON—of those Marine Corps forces and capabilities not designated by the JFC for tasking by functional component commanders. The Marine Corps component commander advises functional component commanders on the most effective use of Marine Corps forces or capabilities made available. Marine Corps forces or capabilities made available by the JFC respond to the functional component commander for operational matters based on the existing command relationship. All Marine Corps forces receive administrative and logistic support from the Marine Corps component commander. The JFC may also establish a support relationship between components to facilitate operations. See MCDP 1-0.1 for more information on the designation and responsibilities of functional component commanders.

Designation of a functional component commander must not affect the command relationships between Service component commanders and the JFC. The JFC must specifically assign the responsibilities and authority of the functional component commander. The JFC defines the responsibilities and authority based on the concept of operations and may alter these responsibilities and authority during the course of an operation. Functional component commander responsibilities are found in JP 0-2 and JP 3-0, *Doctrine for Joint Operations*.

The Marine Corps Component Commander as a Functional Component Commander

Forward-deployed naval forces, including Marine Corps forces, are usually the first conventional forces to arrive in an austere theater or AO during expeditionary operations. The Marine Corps component commander's inherent capability to command and control Marine Corps forces—and attached or assigned forces of other Services or nations—allows him to command and control a functional component. The Marine Corps component commander can serve as a functional component commander in most smaller-scale contingencies and MOOTW. If the Marine Corps component commander is assigned functional component commander responsibilities, execution is normally accomplished by the assigned MAGTF.

As the commander of the force most capable of rapid worldwide deployment, the Marine Corps component commander may serve as a functional component commander in the initial phase of a MTW. As the theater matures and additional US forces flow into the theater, the Marine Corps component commander's capability to command and control these joint forces diminishes. When the functional component commanders establish their headquarters and supporting infrastructure, they begin to assume command and control of their assigned forces and capabilities. The transition of functional component duties from the Marine Corps component commander continues until the gaining functional component commander demonstrates full operational capability. The JFC can designate the Marine Corps component commander as follows.

Joint Force Maritime Component Commander

This commander is responsible for planning, coordinating, and executing joint maritime operations. Joint maritime operations are performed with maritime capabilities or forces made available by components to support the JFC's operation or campaign objectives or to support other components of the joint force. The maritime environment includes oceans, littorals, riverine areas, and amphibious objective areas, and the coordinated airspace above them as defined by the JFC. The joint force commander will designate the component commander best suited to accomplish the mission as the joint force maritime component commander (JFMCC). When maritime operations are focused on littoral operations—and Marine Corps forces have the preponderance of the mission or capabilities to accomplish the mission—the Marine Corps component commander may be designated the JFMCC.

Joint Force Land Component Commander

This commander is responsible for planning, coordinating, and executing joint land operations. Joint land operations are performed with land capabilities or forces made available by components to support the JFCs operation or campaign objectives or to support other components of the joint force. Marine Corps component commanders normally have the preponderance of land forces and the necessary command and control capability to direct their activities during expeditionary operations in a smaller-scale contingency. In the early stages of a MTW, the Marine Corps component commander may serve as the joint force land component commander (JFLCC), but as forces continue to build up in theater, the JFC will normally designate the Army Service component commander as the JFLCC.

Joint Force Air Component Commander

This commander is responsible for planning, coordinating, and executing joint air operations. Joint air operations are performed with air capabilities or forces made available by components to support the JFC's operation or campaign objectives or to support other components of the joint force. The expeditionary nature of

Marine aviation and its associated command and control capability allow the Marine Corps component commander to function as the JFACC in a smaller-scale contingency. In the early stages of an MTW, the Marine Corps component commander may serve as the JFACC, but as forces continue to build up in theater, the JFC will normally designate another component commander as the JFACC. Most often, the JFC conducts operations through a combination of Service and functional component commands with operational responsibilities. Joint forces organized with Army, Navy, Air Force, and Marine Corps components will have special operations forces (if assigned) organized as a functional component. The JFC defines the authority and responsibilities of the Service and functional component commanders. However, the Service responsibilities, e.g., administrative and logistic, of the components must be given due consideration by the JFC. In addition to functional component responsibilities, a JFC can assign the Marine Corps component commander other joint responsibilities. The JFC can designate the Marine Corps component commander as the area air defense commander, airspace control authority, joint rear area coordinator or to establish the joint search and rescue center.

Marine Corps
Core Competencies
● ● ● ● ● ● ●

The Marine Corps' contribution to national security and its role within a naval expeditionary force rest upon five unique core competencies. These competencies define the essence of the Marine Corps' institutional culture and its contribution to the national military establishment. Core competencies are the set of specific capabilities or activities fundamental to a Service or agency role. The Marine Corps' core competencies allow Marines to conduct expeditionary operations across the spectrum of crisis and conflict around the world. These core competencies, articulated by the Commandant of the Marine Corps in *Expeditionary Maneuver Warfare*, follow. (MCDP 1-0)

Warfighting Culture and Dynamic Decisionmaking

War is fundamentally a clash of human wills and, as such, its outcomes are often determined more by human qualities than by technology. For this reason, Marines focus on the force of human resolve and utilize technology to leverage the chaos and complexity of the battlefield. From early on, Marines are instilled with a determination to accomplish the mission, ingeniously adapting available resources in chaotic and austere operating environments to realize success in battle. While Marines leverage technology to enhance tempo and decisionmaking capabilities, their training, education, and experience foster decisiveness even in the absence of perfect information. This "decision superiority" recognizes that technology will never fully obviate fog and friction, and that the human ability to make effective decisions in battle is best achieved by intuition built through rigorous training, practiced discipline, and relevant experience. Leveraging chaos and complexity through information and decisionmaking technologies provides a truly asymmetric advantage to Marines engaged across the spectrum of operations.

Expeditionary Forward Operations

Marines are continuously deployed around the world near potential trouble spots where they can deter aggression, respond quickly, and resolve crises whenever called. The Corps' naval character and its strategically mobile presence enhance cultural and situational awareness of potential operating areas. This enhanced awareness enables Marines to work with friends and allies throughout each region, and is a cornerstone of the combatant commander's engagement plans.

Sustainable and Interoperable Littoral Power Projection

Today's scalable MAGTFs can access the worlds littoral regions on short notice, responding quickly with a force tailored to the mission at hand. Our partnership with the Navy provides significant organic sustainment capabilities from the sea, and reduces the combatant commander's requirement to dedicate precious lift assets to sustaining early entry forces. This means that sustainable and credible naval forces can begin responding to a crisis early, supporting other elements of national power while giving the joint or multinational commander time to develop the theater of operations more fully as required.

Combined Arms Integration

Marines pioneered development of concepts such as close air support and vertical envelopment. MAGTFs constantly blend the art and science of commanding, controlling, training, and executing combined arms operations from air, land, sea, and space. Marines understand the logic and synergy of joint and multinational forces under the "single battle" concept because of their culture and training in combined arms and expeditionary operations. They have experience with other government and nongovernmental agencies. MAGTFs deliver desired "effects" through both lethal and nonlethal means, with simultaneity and depth across the spectrum of operations. Marine employment of combined arms at the tactical level of war is a truly unique capability that reflects our innovative approach to warfighting and complements the tenets of maneuver warfare.

Forcible Entry from the Sea

Together, the Navy and Marine Corps provide the Nation with its primary capability to rapidly project and sustain combat power ashore in the face of armed opposition. When access to safeguarding America's interests is denied or in jeopardy, forward-present, rapidly deployable Marine forces are trained and ready to create and exploit seams in an enemy's defenses by leveraging available joint and naval capabilities, projecting sustainable power ashore, and securing entry for follow-on forces. MEFs, reinforced by maritime prepositioned assets when required, allow the US to protect its worldwide interests, reassure allies, and fortify other elements of national power.

Expeditionary Operations

An expedition is a military operation conducted by an armed force to accomplish a specific objective in a foreign country. Expeditionary operations encompass the entire range of military operations, from foreign humanitarian assistance to forcible entry in an MTW. The defining characteristic of expeditionary operations is the projection of force into a foreign setting. (MCDP 1-0)

Force Projection

Forward-deployed MAGTFs, with their range of capabilities, are designed to enable the JFC to resolve crises and win conflicts. MAGTFs are uniquely suited to support the national security strategy by rapidly projecting the required capability into a foreign setting to abate the crisis. This capability is central to the US's ability to safeguard its national interests. Forward-deployed MAGTFs are prepared to meet a wide array of challenges in their AO. Their presence and engagement activities help to shape the crisis area. Finally, MAGTFs respond with appropriate force or capabilities to defeat the enemy, restore order, or provide humanitarian relief. The Marine Corps conducts force projection primarily through the use of MAGTFs conducting expeditionary operations employing three primary methods (MCDP 1-0):

* Amphibious operations.
* MPF operations.
* Combination of the above methods.

Amphibious Operations

An amphibious operation is a military operation launched from the sea by an amphibious force (AF) embarked in ships or craft with the primary purpose of introducing an LF ashore to accomplish the assigned mission. Amphibious operations require a high degree of training and specialized equipment to succeed. Marine Corps forces are specifically organized, trained, and equipped to deploy aboard, operate from, and sustain themselves from amphibious ships. They are specifically designed to project land combat power ashore from the sea. Types of amphibious operations include assaults, withdrawals, demonstrations, raids, and other amphibious operations in a permissive, uncertain, or hostile environment. An AF conducts amphibious operations. (JP 3-02)

- An AF is an amphibious task force (ATF) and an LF, together with other forces that are trained, organized, and equipped for amphibious operations.

- An ATF is a Navy task organization formed to conduct amphibious operations.

- An LF is a Marine Corps or Army task organization formed to conduct amphibious operations.

The terms "commander, amphibious task force" (CATF) and "commander, landing force" (CLF) are solely to clarify the doctrinal duties and responsibilities of these commanders. In operations and exercises, amphibious commanders are referred to by either their operational command titles (i.e., Commanding

General, 2d Marine Expeditionary Brigade [CG2d MEB]),
Commander, Amphibious Group TWO [CPG 2]) or assigned task
force designators (e.g., Combined Task Force [CTF] 62.1), not by
the terms "CATF" or "CLF." The terms "CATF" and "CLF" do
not connote titles or command relationships.

Amphibious Operation Command Relationships

Command relationships in amphibious operations should facilitate cooperative planning between the joint force, the Navy; and
the Marine forces. They should ensure that appropriate responsibility and authority for the conduct of the amphibious operation
is assigned to the commander of the Marine forces. The command
relationship options available to a JFC or other establishing
authority of an amphibious operation include OPCON, TACON,
and support as described in JP 0-2 and JP 3-02, *Joint Doctrine for
Amphibious Operations*. While doctrine should not specify a
normal command relationship, typically a support relationship is
established between the ATF commander (Navy) and the LF
commander (Marine or Army) based on the complementary
capabilities of the ATF and the LF.

Control of Amphibious Forces

The JFC will organize the AF in such a way as to best accomplish
the mission based on the concept of operations.

- If conducting operations through the Service components, the
  JFC may establish a support relationship between the Navy
  component commander and the Service component
  commander of the LF, or delegate OPCON or TACON of the
  assigned or attached AFs to a Service component.

- If conducting operations through a combination of Service and
  functional component commands with operational responsibilities, the JFC may establish a support relationship between the

functional components, Service components, or other appropriate commanders, or delegate OPCON or TACON of the assigned or attached AFs to a functional component or Service component commander. Normally, joint forces are organized with a combination of Service and functional component commands with operational responsibilities.

Operational Control

The establishing authority may choose to delegate OPCON to a single commander within the AF. When OPCON is delegated, it will include the following authority (in accordance with JP 0-2) unless otherwise specified.

* Exercise or delegate OPCON and TACON, establish support relationships among subordinates, and designate coordinating authorities.

* Give direction to subordinate commands and forces necessary to carry out missions assigned to the command, including authoritative direction over all aspects of the amphibious operation and training.

* Prescribe the chain of command to the commands and forces within the command.

* Organize commands and employ forces within the AF, as necessary, to carry out assigned missions.

* Employ forces within the command, as necessary, to carry out missions assigned to the command.

* Assign command functions to subordinate commanders.

* Plan for, deploy, direct, control, and coordinate the action of subordinate forces.

* Establish plans, policies, priorities, and overall requirements for the intelligence activities of the command.

- Suspend from duty subordinate commanders and recommend reassignment of any officer assigned to the command.

- Assign responsibilities to subordinate commanders for certain routine operational matters that require coordination of effort of two or more commanders.

- Establish an adequate system of control for local defense and delineate such areas of operation for subordinate commanders as deemed desirable.

- Delineate functional responsibilities and geographic areas of operation of subordinate commanders.

OPCON normally provides full authority to organize commands and forces and employ those forces as the commander in OPCON considers necessary to accomplish assigned missions. It does not, in and of itself, include authoritative direction for logistics or matters of administration, discipline, internal organization, or unit training.

Tactical Control

TACON is the command authority over assigned or attached forces or commands (or military capability or forces made available for tasking) that is limited to the detailed and usually local direction and control of movements or maneuvers necessary to accomplish assigned missions or tasks. The establishing authority may choose to delegate TACON to a single commander within the amphibious force. When TACON is delegated, it will include the following authority (in accordance with JP 0-2) unless otherwise specified.

- Give direction for specified military operations.
- Control designated forces.

TACON does not provide organizational authority or authoritative direction for administrative and logistic support; the commander of the parent unit continues to exercise these authorities unless otherwise specified in the establishing directive.

Support

Support is a command authority. The establishing authority of the amphibious operation establishes a support relationship between commanders within the amphibious force as well as other designated commanders as appropriate. This relationship is appropriate when one organization should aid, protect, complement, or sustain another force. The designation of the supporting relationships is important as it conveys priorities to the commanders and staffs who are planning or executing the operation. The support relationship is, by design, a somewhat vague and therefore very flexible arrangement. This flexibility is enhanced by the publishing of an establishing directive to specify the purpose of the support, the desired effect, and the scope of action to be taken.

Supported Commander

A supported commander may be designated for the entire operation, a particular phase or stage of the operation, a particular function, or a combination of phases, stages, events, and functions. Unless limited by the establishing directive or the order initiating the amphibious operation, the supported commander has the authority to exercise general direction of the supporting effort. General direction includes the designation and prioritization of targets or objectives, timing and duration of the supporting action, and other instructions necessary for coordination and efficiency. The establishing authority is responsible for ensuring that the supported and supporting commanders understand the degree of authority that the supported commander is granted.

* If not specified in the order initiating the amphibious operation, the CATF and CLF will determine who has primary responsibility for the essential tasks during the mission analysis in the planning process.

* In an operation of relatively short duration, normally the establishing authority will choose one commander for the entire operation. When there is no littoral threat to the amphibious force (for example, in a particular noncombatant evacuation operation) the establishing authority may designate the CLF as the supported commander for the entire operation. During the movement or transit phase, the CATF may be designated the supported commander based on having responsibility for the major action or activity during that phase. The CATF may be designated the supported commander based on capabilities for airspace control and air defense for the entire operation if, for example, the LF does not intend to establish a tactical air command center ashore.

* The establishing authority should consider several factors when designating the supported commander at various phases and events during the amphibious operation, including but not limited to the following.
    ** Responsibility for the preponderance of the mission.
    ** Force capabilities.
    ** Threat.
    ** Type, phase, and duration of operation.
    ** Command and control capabilities.
    ** Battlespace assigned.
    ** Recommendations from subordinate commanders.

Supporting Commander

The supporting commander determines the forces, tactics, methods, procedures, and communications to be employed in providing support to the supported commander. The supporting commander will advise and coordinate with the supported commander on matters concerning the employment and limitations (e.g., logistics) of such support, assist in planning for the integration of such support into the supported commander's effort as a whole, and ensure that support requirements are appropriately communicated throughout the supporting commander's organization. The supporting commander has the responsibility to ascertain the needs of the supported force and take full action to fulfill them within existing capabilities, consistent with priorities and requirements of other assigned tasks. When the supporting commander cannot fulfill the needs of the supported commander, the establishing authority will be notified by either the supported or supporting commander. The establishing authority is responsible for determining a solution.

Parallel Chains of Command

Elements of the AF (ATF, LF, and other forces) may be embarked for what could be extended periods of time on the same platforms, but responsible to different or parallel chains of command. Such parallel chains of command create special requirements for coordination. Except in emergencies, no significant decision contemplated by a commander in the chain of command that affects the plans, disposition, or intentions of a corresponding commander in another chain of command will be made without consultation with the commander concerned. In emergency situations, the commander making an emergency decision will notify corresponding commanders of his or her action at the earliest practicable time.

Phases

The five phases of an amphibious operation, as delineated in
JP 3-02, are always required, but their sequence may change as
circumstances dictate.

Planning. The planning phase normally denotes the period
extending from the issuance of an order that directs the operation
to take place and ends with the embarkation of LFs. Planning,
however, is continuous throughout the operation. Although
planning does not cease with the termination of this phase, it is
useful to distinguish between the planning phase and subsequent
phases because of the change that may occur in the relationship
between AF commanders when the planning phase ends and the
operational phase begins.

Embarkation. The embarkation phase is when the LFs, with their
equipment and supplies, embark in assigned shipping. Organization for embarkation needs to provide for flexibility to support
changes to the original plan. The landing plan and scheme of
maneuver ashore are based on conditions and enemy capabilities
existing in the operational area before embarkation of the LF. A
change in conditions of friendly or enemy forces during the
movement phase may cause changes in either plan with no opportunity for reconfiguration of the LF. The extent to which changes
in the landing plan can be accomplished may depend on the
ability to reconfigure embarked forces.

Rehearsal. Rehearsal may consist of an actual landing or may be
conducted as a command post exercise. The rehearsal phase is
when the prospective operation is rehearsed to—

- Test the adequacy of plans, timing of detailed operations, and
combat readiness of participating forces.
- Ensure that all echelons are familiar with plans.

- Provide an opportunity to reconfigure embarked forces and equipment.
- Verify communications for commonality, redundancy, security, and reliability.

Movement. The movement phase is when various elements of the AF move from points of embarkation or from a forward-deployed position to the operational area. This move may be via rehearsal, staging, or rendezvous areas. The movement phase is completed when the various elements of the AF arrive at their assigned positions in the operational area.

Action. The decisive action phase is the period from the arrival of the AF in the operational area through the accomplishment of the mission to the termination of the amphibious operation. While planning occurs throughout the entire operation, it is normally dominant prior to embarkation. Successive phases bear the title of the dominant activity taking place within the phase.

Maritime Prepositioning Force

The MPF is an integral part of the Marine Corps' expeditionary capability. Rapid response to regional contingencies is its primary role. An MPF consists of the MPS squadron (MPSRON), Navy support element, and MAGTF fly-in echelon. Together they provide the JFC with a proven, flexible force that can quickly respond to a full range of missions from combat to humanitarian relief. Fundamental to the MPF is its interoperability with joint forces and its rapid introduction of combat forces into austere environments. (MCDP 1-0)

Comprised of specially designed ships, organized into three squadrons, MPSRONs carry equipment and supplies for 30 days of combat operations by a MEB of approximately 16,000 Marines and Sailors. When deployed together, these squadrons provide equipment and supplies to support a MEF. These squadrons are forward-deployed to ensure rapid closure to the crisis area within a 5- to 14-day sailing period. MAGTF and Navy support element personnel are airlifted to a previously seized lodgment, a benign or host nation port and airfield, or to an intermediate support base where they link up with equipment and supplies offloaded from the MPSRON. If a port is not available, the squadron may be offloaded in-stream. A unique characteristic of the MPF is that the embarked equipment is maintained aboard ship and is combat-ready immediately upon offload. The entire squadron or selected capability sets from designated ships can be offloaded to support a wide range of MAGTF missions.

Battlespace Organization

Understanding the joint battlespace at the operational level of war in which Marine Corps forces will operate is an important step in setting the conditions for their success. Marines must understand the relationship between the AO, area of interest, and area of influence. By analyzing the AO in terms of the area of influence and area of interest, a Marine commander determines whether the assigned AO is appropriate. This analysis may include the forces' capabilities to conduct actions across the warfighting functions. The size of these areas and the types of forces employed within them depend on the scope and nature of the crisis and the projected duration of the operation. Battlespace is normally comprised of an AO, area of influence, and area of interest. (MCDP 1-0)

Area of Operations

An AO is an operational area defined by the JFC for land and naval forces. AOs do not typically encompass the entire operational area of the JFC, but should be large enough for the Marine Corps component commander and the subordinate units to accomplish their missions and protect their forces. The AO is the tangible area of battlespace and is the only area of battlespace that a commander is directly responsible for. AOs should also be large enough to allow commanders to employ their organic, assigned, and supporting systems to the limits of their capabilities. The commander must be able to command and control all the forces within the AO. The commander must be able to see the entire AO—this includes coverage of the AO with the full range of collections assets and sensors available to the Marine Corps component command and MAGTF, to include reconnaissance, electronic warfare aircraft, unmanned aerial vehicles, remote sensors, and radars. The commander must be able to control the events and coordinate his subordinates' actions. Finally, the commander must be able to strike and maneuver throughout the AO.

Amphibious Objective Area

An amphibious objective area is a geographical area (delineated for command and control purposes in the order initiating the amphibious operation) within which is located the objective(s) to be secured by the amphibious force. This area must be of sufficient size to ensure accomplishment of the amphibious force's mission and must provide sufficient area for conducting necessary sea, air, and land operations. (JP 3-02)

Area of Influence

The area of influence is that geographical area wherein a commander is directly capable of influencing operations by maneuver or fire support systems normally under the commander's command or control. It is that portion of the battlespace that the commander can affect through the maneuver, fires, and other actions of the force. Its size is normally based on the limits of organic systems (fire support, aviation, mobility, and reconnaissance capabilities) and operational requirements identified within each of the warfighting functions. The area of influence normally reflects the extent of the force's operational reach. MAGTFs have significant areas of influence, employing Marine fixed-wing aviation, to extend the operational reach of Marine forces.

Area of Interest

The area of interest contains friendly and enemy forces, capabilities, infrastructure, and terrain that concern the commander. This area includes the area of influence and those areas that contain current or planned objectives or enemy forces that are capable of endangering mission accomplishment. The size of the area of interest normally exceeds the commander's operational reach. See figure 5.

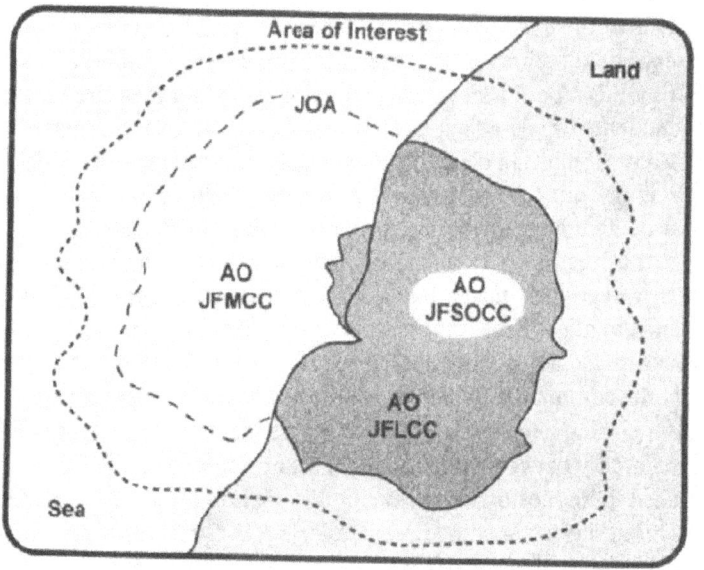

Figure 5. Area of Interest.

Control Measures

Commanders at the operational level of war use control measures to control and coordinate the operations of their forces in the battlespace. Two frequently used control measures are the fire support coordination line (FSCL) and high-density airspace control zone (HIDACZ).

Fire Support Coordination Line

One of the most important and frequently misused fire support coordinating measures at the operational level is the FSCL. A FSCL is a permissive fire support coordinating measure used to facilitate timely attack of the enemy by air and surface-based fires. Supporting elements may engage targets beyond the FSCL without prior coordination with the establishing commander, provided the attack will not produce adverse effects on or to the rear of the FSCL or on forces operating beyond the FSCL. However, they must inform all affected commanders in sufficient time to allow necessary reaction to avoid fratricide. It is established and adjusted by the appropriate ground or amphibious force commander in consultation with superior, subordinate, supporting, and other affected commanders. The FSCL is not a boundary between aviation and ground forces and should not be used to delineate a de facto AO for aviation forces. It is located within the establishing commander's AO. Synchronization of operations on either side of the FSCL out to the forward boundary of the establishing unit is the responsibility of the establishing commander. When possible the FSCL should be drawn along readily identifiable terrain to aid in recognition. (MCDP 1-0)

High-Density Airspace Control Zone

A HIDACZ is airspace designated in an airspace control plan or airspace control order in which there is a concentrated employment of numerous and varied weapons and airspace users.

A HIDACZ has defined dimensions that usually coincide with geographical features or navigational aids. Access to a HIDACZ is normally controlled by the maneuver commander. The maneuver commander can also direct a more restrictive weapons status within the HIDACZ. (JP 3-02)

The Marine Corps Planning Process

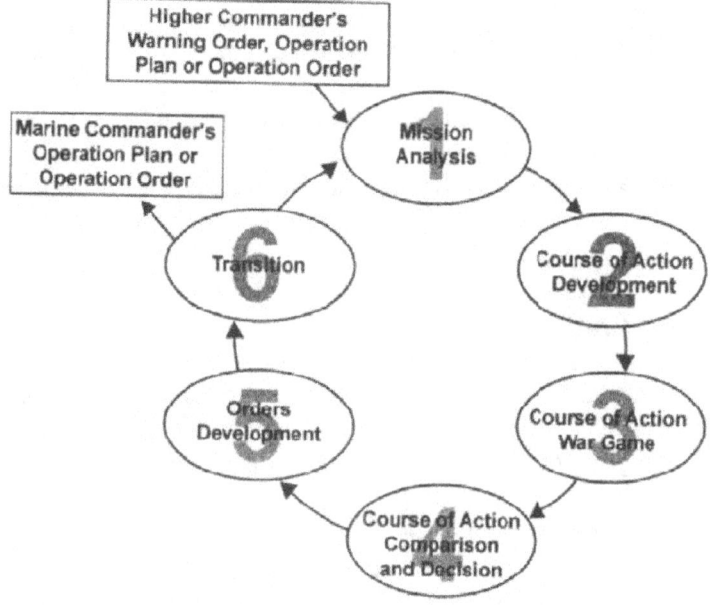

Figure 6. Steps in the Marine Corps Planning Process.

The Marine Corps Planning Process (see fig. 6) establishes procedures for analyzing a mission, developing and wargaming
courses of action (COAs) against the threat, comparing friendly
COAs against the commander's criteria and each other, selecting

a COA, preparing an operation order (OPORD) or operation plan (OPLAN) for execution, and transitioning the order or plan to those tasked with its execution. The Marine Corps Planning Process organizes these procedures into six manageable, logical steps.

These steps provide the commander and the staff, at all levels, a means to organize their planning activities, to transmit plans to subordinates and subordinate commands, and to share a common understanding of the mission and commander's intent. Interactions among various planning steps allow a concurrent, coordinated effort that maintains flexibility, makes efficient use of time available, and facilitates continuous information sharing. See Marine Corps Warfighting Publication (MCWP) 5-1, *Marine Corps Planning Process*, appendix C for further information on organizing the planning effort.

Mission Analysis

Mission analysis is the first step in planning, and it drives the Marine Corps Planning Process. Its purpose is to review and analyze orders, guidance, and other information provided by higher headquarters and to produce a unit mission statement.

Course of Action Development

During COA development, planners use the mission statement (which includes the higher headquarters commander's tasking and intent), commander's intent, and commander's planning guidance to develop COA(s). Each prospective COA is examined to ensure that it is suitable, feasible, acceptable, distinguishable, and complete with respect to the current and anticipated situation, the mission, and the commander's intent.

Course of Action War Game

Course of action wargaming involves a detailed assessment of each COA as it pertains to the enemy and the battlespace. Each friendly COA is wargamed against selected threat COAs. Course of action wargaming assists planners in identifying strengths and weaknesses, associated risks, and asset shortfalls for each friendly COA. Course of action wargaming also identifies branches and potential sequels that may require additional planning. Short of actually executing the course of action, COA wargaming provides the most reliable basis for understanding and improving each COA.

Course of Action Comparison and Decision

In COA comparison and decision, the commander evaluates all friendly COAs against established criteria, then evaluates them against each other. The commander then selects the COA that will best accomplish the mission.

Orders Development

During orders development, the staff uses the commander's COA decision, mission statement, and commander's intent and guidance to develop orders that direct unit actions. Orders serve as the principal means by which the commander expresses the commander's decision, intent, and guidance.

Transition

Transition is an orderly handover of a plan or order as it is passed to those tasked with execution of the operation. It provides those who will execute the plan or order with the situational awareness and rationale for key decisions necessary to ensure there is a coherent shift from planning to execution.

MCPP Compared with Other
Services and Joint Planning Processes

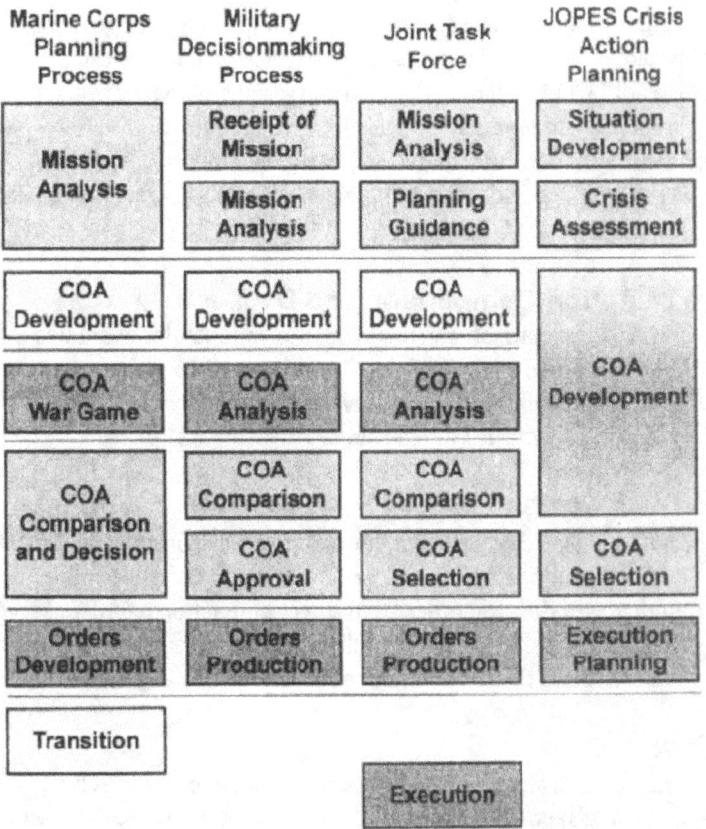

Marine Corps Planning Process	Military Decisionmaking Process	Joint Task Force	JOPES Crisis Action Planning
Mission Analysis	Receipt of Mission	Mission Analysis	Situation Development
	Mission Analysis	Planning Guidance	Crisis Assessment
COA Development	COA Development	COA Development	COA Development
COA War Game	COA Analysis	COA Analysis	
COA Comparison and Decision	COA Comparison	COA Comparison	
	COA Approval	COA Selection	COA Selection
Orders Development	Orders Production	Orders Production	Execution Planning
Transition			
		Execution	

NOTE: Like steps of each planning process are colored in the same manner.

Figure 7. Comparison of the Planning Process.

Figure 7 shows the comparison between the Marine Corps Planning Process with the other Services and joint planning processes. Although there may be minor nuances between these processes (such as what the step is called or which step a particular process falls into), overall the processes are the same. If you know and understand the Marine Corps Planning Process, you are well suited to be a member of any planning group at any level.

Rapid Planning

The goal of rapid planning is to expend less time planning in order to provide the executing forces with the maximum time allowable to prepare for the mission. Rapid planning conducted by well-trained, experienced commanders and their staffs can create a tempo of operations that overwhelm the enemy and achieve the commander's objectives. But, hastily conceived, ill-considered plans probably won't succeed, and could result in death. Therefore, the commander and the staff must achieve balance between sufficient time to develop a feasible COA, sufficient time to coordinate its critical details, and sufficient time to prepare for its execution. The commander and the staff must be thoroughly familiar with potential contingencies or missions, and every individual involved with planning must know his or her role in the planning process. Successful rapid planning is predicated on the unit's early retrieval or receipt of sufficient intelligence and related information; planning experience; foresight to make significant preparations in organizing, training, and equipping; information management; and highly refined, well-rehearsed standing operating procedures (SOPs). If rapid planning is successful, both planning and preparation requirements are conducted concurrently. The speed in which a unit can plan an operation varies with the complexity of the mission, the experience of the commander and the staff, and mission, enemy, terrain and weather, troops and support available—time available (METT-T) factors. If time does not allow use of the full, six-step

Marine Corps Planning Process, then the commander and the planners may use the rapid response planning process (R2P2), which is a time-constrained version of the full planning process. The R2P2 was developed to enable the MEU(SOC) to plan and begin execution of certain tasks within a 6-hour time period. The rapid planning techniques focus on the MEU(SOC) and its 6-hour timeline, but these techniques may be tailored and employed to meet any unit's needs. Rapid planning by non-MEU(SOC) units is usually more effective when conducting routine missions, standard missions, or tasks for which the unit has been well-trained and has established SOPs. (MCWP 5-1)

Actions Prior to Rapid Planning

To best employ R2P2, a unit must develop capabilities in four areas: planning cells, planning and operations SOPs, intelligence, and information management. If one of these areas is lacking, effective rapid planning may not be achieved.

Planning Cells

The amount of staff turnover in the planning cells, to include the commander, directly impacts the staff's ability to plan rapidly; therefore, the composition and membership of the various planning cells used in rapid planning should remain standard. This is particularly true during the predeployment training program and deployment of the MEU(SOC) and amphibious squadron (PHIBRON). The planning cells employed by the MEU(SOC) and PHIBRON usually include the crisis action team (CAT), the battle staff, and the mission planning cells. These cells must participate in frequent planning exercises that involve real-world scenarios similar to those the unit might encounter. These exercises ensure that the CAT, battle staff, and mission planning cells are thoroughly trained in rapid planning; their members know their commanders and each other; and the planners possess situational awareness of likely contingency missions and AOs. Planning cells should understand where they are to meet, what they are to accomplish, and how much time they have to complete their planning efforts. The planning cells also must be capable of conducting concurrent (simultaneous at different echelons of the same command) and parallel (between equivalent echelons of different commands) planning.

Planning and Operations SOPs

SOPs are the cornerstone of rapid planning. The planning SOP should be second nature to all concerned. Operations SOPs are equally important because they allow planners to select proven and practiced tasks that provide solutions to tactical problems. SOPs allow major subordinate elements (MSEs) to carry out familiar tasks effectively and efficiently with minimal or no higher-level guidance or communications. The SOP for each type of mission should include a predesignated task organization; equipment and ordnance lists; elements of a landing plan; mission execution procedures; and an execution checklist with codewords. The SOPs must be studied, rehearsed, executable on a moment's notice, and supported by timesaving factors. For example, standard ordnance packages for likely missions (e.g., tactical recovery of aircraft and personnel [TRAP], platoon-size reinforcements) are prestaged in readily accessible locations in their magazines in order to reduce the time needed to break out and issue ammunition. In addition, mission smart packs are created for each mission profile. Smart packs contain specific planning information and SOPs based on the mission profile (e.g., light, medium, or heavy helicopter raid). Smart pack planning and coordination of information are also used as references during mission execution.

Intelligence

The commander and the staff must anticipate possible contingencies based on continual analyses of open-source news and classified intelligence reports. For each situation, the staff should be equipped with the latest intelligence (e.g., a MEU[SOC] usually prepares mission folders), possible targets, area studies, and other relevant information. Periodic reviews of potential contingencies maintain situational awareness and assist in updating information. When appropriate, a commander conducts deliberate planning and refocuses unit training based on likely scenarios. The intelligence staff must also be familiar with the *Generic Intelligence Requirements Handbook*, which is produced by Marine Corps Intelligence Activity. The *Generic Intelligence Requirements Handbook* contains suggested essential elements of information for various mission types.

Information Management

Due to the time constraints inherent in rapid planning, there is less opportunity for the commander and the staff to analyze information requirements. Also, computer technology is increasing the speed and volume of information flow, so an overabundance of information may obscure vital facts. It is critical that every participant in the planning process realizes the importance of the mission area and take positive steps to appropriately share knowledge. Commanders and staff officers must possess the ability to present clear and concise information. Simple, concise presentations best support rapid planning.

Composition of MEU(SOC) Planning Cells
Crisis Action Team
The central planning cell in the MEU(SOC) and PHIBRON is the CAT. Although its final composition depends on the commander and METT-T, its basic composition is established in the

command SOP. Three factors to consider in determining membership in the CAT are the physical space available to accommodate the group, the benefits of additional input from a wider array of functional areas, and the drawbacks of too many participants. CAT members of a MEU(SOC) may include the MEU(SOC) and PHIBRON commanders and their primary staffs, MSE commanders and their operations officers, and subject matter experts.

> **NOTE:** Some MEU(SOC)s interchangeably refer to the CAT or the LF operations center watch team as the battle staff.

Battle Staff
Some MEU(SOC) and PHIBRON commanders employ a battle staff. The battle staff may consist of staff officers at the MEU(SOC) and PHIBRON and MSE level, plus representatives from attachments and functional areas not included in the CAT. Ideally, any potential member of a mission planning cell not part of the CAT should be on the battle staff. The battle staff convenes whenever the CAT is established, which provides leaders and planners an opportunity to gain identical situational awareness with the CAT and to prepare for participation in any mission planning cell. Because there are insufficient personnel in some functional areas to staff all mission planning cells simultaneously, the battle staff may have members that support more than one mission planning cell.

Mission Planning Cell
Early in the planning process, the MEU(SOC) and PHIBRON commanders designate a mission commander (usually one of the MSE commanders or the maritime special purpose force commander). The mission commander then establishes his or her own mission planning cell to plan the details of the operation. Consideration must be given to the feasibility of separate

planning cells due to limited staff members; therefore, the mission commander may designate more than one planning cell in order to plan concurrent, contingency, or follow-on missions. Additionally, a separate reconnaissance and surveillance mission planning cell may be established to plan reconnaissance and surveillance operations. Each mission planning cell should include appropriate representation from relevant experts (e.g., a battalion landing team planning cell might include air and logistic subject matter experts and Navy representatives). Maintaining the same personnel in the planning cells throughout the work-up and deployment speeds and improves the planning process (e.g., if the ACE is the primary mission commander for a TRAP, then the GCE should send the same representative to all TRAP planning meetings). The planning cell's working spaces must be predesignated so that all cell members know where to report and so that two cells are not competing for the same space. Lower echelon units, such as companies and platoons, must be prepared to plan concurrently with the mission planning cells and also have a designated planning space.

MEU(SOC) Rapid Response Planning Process

R2P2 is a time-constrained, six step process that mirrors the Marine Corps Planning Process of—

- Mission analysis.
- COA development.
- COA war game.
- COA comparison and decision.
- Orders development.
- Transition.

The MAGTF Liaison Officer
• • • • • • •

Liaison is the contact or intercommunication maintained between elements of military forces to ensure understanding and unity of purpose and action. Liaison helps to reduce the fog of war through direct communications. It ensures that senior commanders remain aware of the tactical situation by providing them with exceptional, critical, or routine information; verification of information; and clarification of operational questions. Overall, liaison is another tool to help commanders overcome friction and accomplish their mission.

The liaison officer is the most commonly used means of maintaining close, continuous contact with another command. He is the commander's personal representative. He has the special trust and confidence of the commander to make appropriate recommendations and estimates in the absence of communications. As necessary, the commander uses a liaison officer to transmit or receive critical information directly with key persons in the receiving headquarters. The liaison officer must possess the requisite rank and experience to properly represent his command. The ability to communicate effectively is essential, as is sound judgment. Equally, he must have immediate access to his commander. (MCWP 5-1).

The commander uses a liaison officer to transmit critical information while bypassing layers of staffs and headquarters. A trained, competent, trusted, and informed liaison officer (either an officer or a noncommissioned officer) is the key to effective liaison. The liaison officer must have the proper rank and experience for the mission and have the commander's full confidence. When interfacing with joint and multinational forces, rank may need to be increased to enhance accessibility and influence. Employing one individual conserves manpower while guaranteeing the consistent, accurate flow of information. However, continuous operations require a liaison team.

The liaison officer normally is a special staff officer. He is the personal representative of the commander and has access to his commander consistent with his duties. However, for routine matters, he works for and receives direction from the chief of staff (or executive officer). The liaison officer's parent unit is the sending unit; the unit the liaison officer visits or is attached to is the receiving unit. A liaison officer normally remains at the receiving headquarters until recalled to the sending unit. Because the liaison officer represents his commander, he must be able to—

- Understand how his commander thinks.
- Interpret his commander's messages.
- Convey his commander's vision, mission, and concept of operations and guidance.
- Represent his commander's position.

The liaison officer's professional capabilities and personal characteristics must encourage confidence and cooperation with the commander and staff of the receiving unit. He must—

- Be thoroughly knowledgeable of his unit's mission and its tactics, techniques, and procedures; organization; capabilities; and communications equipment.

- Be familiar with the doctrine and staff procedures of the receiving unit's headquarters.

- Appreciate and understand the receiving unit's procedures, organization, capabilities, mission, and customs. (In the case of multinational forces, understanding the unit's doctrine is critical.)

- Be familiar with the requirements for and the purpose of liaison; the liaison system, and its corresponding reports, reporting documents, and records; and the training of the liaison team.

- Observe the established channels of command and staff functions.

- Be of sufficient rank to effectively represent his commander with the receiving unit's commander and staff.

- Be trained in his functional area.

- Possess tact.

- Possess the necessary language expertise, if required.

- Be prepared for and have the capability and resources for sustained operations.

Emerging Concepts and Technologies

Concepts enable decisionmakers the ability to identify capabilities and changes to doctrine, organization, training, and education to create a force for the future. Services and the joint community have relied increasingly on operational concepts as the "engines" for their combat development processes. These concepts also furnish the intellectual basis for experimentation and force development. (MCDP 1-0)

Expeditionary Maneuver Warfare

Expeditionary maneuver warfare is the Marine Corps capstone concept. It prepares the Marine Corps as a "total force in readiness" to meet the challenges and opportunities of a rapidly changing world. Expeditionary maneuver warfare focuses our core competencies, evolving capabilities, and innovative concepts to ensure that the Marine Corps provides the JFC with forces optimized for forward presence, engagement, crisis response, and warfighting. Expeditionary maneuver warfare serves as the basis for influencing the Joint Concept Development and Experimentation Process and the Marine Corps Expeditionary Force Development System. It further refines the broad "axis of advance" identified in *Marine Corps Strategy 21* for future capability enhancements. In doing so, expeditionary maneuver warfare focuses on—

* Joint/multinational enabling. Marine forces are ready to serve as the lead elements of a joint force, act as joint enablers and/or serve as joint task force or functional component commanders (JFLCC, JFACC or JFMCC).

* Strategic agility. Ready forces that are agile, lethal, swift in deployment, and always prepared to move directly to the scene of an emergency or conflict.

* Operational reach. Projecting and sustaining relevant and effective power across the depth of the battlespace.

* Tactical flexibility. Operating with tempo and speed and bringing multirole flexibility (air, land, and sea) to the joint team.

* Support and sustainment. Providing focused logistics to enable power projection independent of host-nation support and against distant objectives across the breadth and depth of a theater of operations.

These capabilities enhance the joint force's ability to reassure and encourage friends and allies while deterring, mitigating, or resolving crises through speed, stealth, and precision. Expeditionary maneuver warfare focuses our warfighting concepts toward realizing the *Marine Corps Strategy 21* vision of future Marine forces with enhanced expeditionary power projection capabilities. It links Marine Corps concepts and vision for integration with emerging joint concepts. As our capstone concept, expeditionary maneuver warfare will guide the process of change to ensure that Marine forces remain *ready, relevant,* and *fully capable* of supporting future joint operations.

Operational Maneuver From the Sea

Operational maneuver from the sea (OMFTS) applies across the range of military operations, from MTW to smaller-scale contingencies. OMFTS applies maneuver warfare to expeditionary power projection in naval operations as part of a joint or multinational campaign. OMFTS allows the force to exploit the sea as maneuver space while applying combat power ashore to achieve the operational objectives. It reflects the Marine Corps' expeditionary maneuver warfare concept in the context of amphibious operations from a seabase, as it enables the force to—

- Shatter the enemy's cohesion.
- Pose menacing dilemmas.
- Apply disruptive firepower.
- Establish superior tempo.
- Focus efforts to maximize effect.
- Exploit opportunity.
- Strike unexpectedly.

The force focuses on an operational objective, using the sea as maneuver space to generate overwhelming tempo and momentum against enemy critical vulnerabilities. OMFTS provides increased operational flexibility through enhanced capabilities for seabased logistics, fires, and command and control. Seabasing facilitates maneuver warfare by eliminating the requirement for an operational pause as the LF builds combat power ashore and by freeing the MAGTF from the constraints of a traditional beachhead. OMFTS is based on six principles:

- *Focus on the Operational Objective.* The operation must be viewed as a continuous event from the port of embarkation to the operational objective ashore. Everything the force does must be focused on achieving the objective of the operation and accomplishing the mission. Intermediate objectives or establishing lodgments ashore assume less importance in OMFTS as the force is centered on decisive maneuver to seize the force objective.

- *Use the Sea as Maneuver Space.* Naval forces use the sea to their advantage, using the sea as an avenue of approach and as a barrier to the enemy's movement. This allows the force to strike unexpectedly anywhere in the littorals and to use deception to mislead the enemy as to actual point of attack.

- *Generate Overwhelming Tempo and Momentum.* The objective of maneuver warfare is to create a tempo greater than that of the enemy. The tempo generated through maneuver from the sea provides the commander freedom of action while limiting the enemy's freedom of action.

- *Pit Friendly Strength Against Enemy Weakness.* The commander identifies and attacks critical vulnerabilities where the enemy is weak, rather than attacking the center of gravity when it is strong.

- *Emphasize Intelligence, Deception, and Flexibility.* Deception enhances force protection while reconnaissance and intelligence are essential in identifying fleeting opportunities.

- *Integrate all Organic, Joint, and Multinational Assets.* To realize the maximum effectiveness the commander must ensure the coordinated use of all available forces and capabilities.

When operating as part of a naval expeditionary force, MEFs will normally focus on conducting operations using OMFTS. The Marine commander, in concert with the Navy counterpart and higher-level direction, will orchestrate the employment of amphibious forces, MPFs, and Marine forces operating from land bases to shape events and create favorable conditions for future combat actions. The amphibious forces will normally execute tactical-level maneuver from the sea to achieve decisive action in battle. For the action to be decisive, the battle must lead to the achievement of the operational objectives.

Ship-to-Objective Maneuver

Ship-to-objective maneuver (STOM) is the tactical implementation of OMFTS by the MAGTF to achieve the JFC's operational objectives. It is the application of maneuver warfare to amphibious operations at the tactical level of war. See figure 8. STOM treats the sea as maneuver space, using the sea as both a protective barrier and an unrestricted avenue of approach. While the aim of ship-to-shore movement was to secure a beachhead, STOM thrusts Marine Corps forces ashore at multiple points to

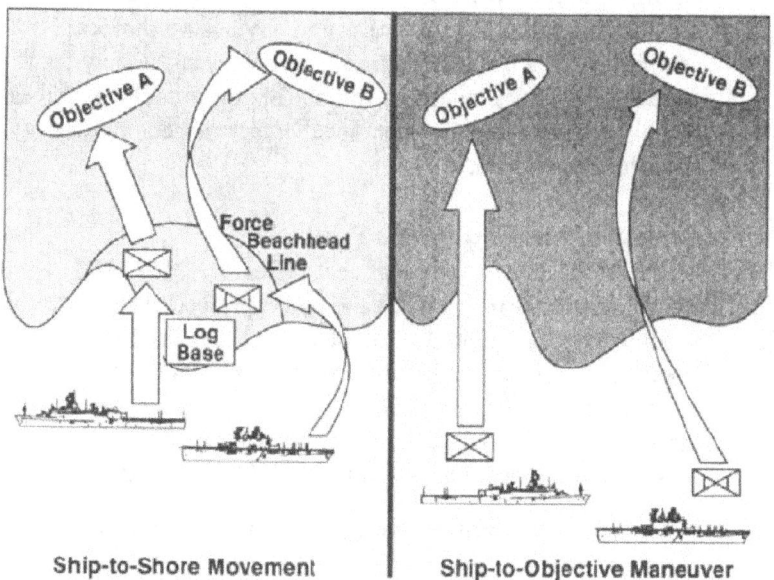

Ship-to-Shore Movement   Ship-to-Objective Maneuver

Figure 8. Operational Objectives.

concentrate at the decisive place and time in sufficient strength to enable success. This creates multiple dilemmas too numerous for the enemy's commander to respond to, disrupting his cohesiveness and diminishing his will or capacity to resist. This concept focuses the force on the operational objective, providing increased flexibility to strike the enemy's critical vulnerabilities. Seabasing of some of the fire support and much of the logistics support reduces the footprint of forces ashore while maintaining the tempo of operations. Emerging command and control capabilities will allow commanders to control the maneuver of their units the moment they cross the line of departure at sea, to include changing the axis of advance or points where they cross the beach during the assault. In STOM, rather than an amphibious assault to establish a force on a hostile or potentially hostile shore, an amphibious attack may occur. An amphibious attack may be defined as an attack launched from the sea by amphibious forces directly against an enemy operational or tactical center of gravity or critical vulnerability.

Maritime Prepositioning Force Future

MPF Future is the concept that next-generation MPFs will contribute to forward presence and power projection capabilities, which will remain central to US deterrence and conflict resolution strategies well into the future. Enhancements envisioned in MPF Future will expand the use of the future MPF across an increased range of contingencies. The concept is best illustrated through the pillars of future MPF operations:

- Force closure—provides for at-sea arrival and assembly of forces.
- Amphibious force integration—using selective offload capabilities to reinforce the assault echelon of an AF.

- Indefinite sustainment—by serving as a seabased conduit for logistic support.

- Reconstitution and redeployment—without a requirement for extensive material maintenance or replenishment at a strategic sustainment base.

Expeditionary Bases and Sites

Future contingencies will compel an ever-increasing reliance on expeditionary bases and sites, especially seabasing, to support and sustain expeditionary maneuver warfare. Expeditionary bases and sites are locations in and out of the AO that can support the deployment, employment, and sustainment of expeditionary forces. They might include—

- Intermediate staging bases outside of the AO.

- Sites located within friendly contiguous nations or the host nation.

- Expeditionary airfields and forward operating bases established within the AO by the expeditionary forces.

- Existing facilities within the AO seized from the enemy.

- US military bases overseas or in CONUS located near the AO.

- Amphibious shipping.

- MPSRONs.

Marine Corps forces can quickly establish these temporary and often austere expeditionary bases and sites providing the ability to project, support, and sustain forces. Amphibious shipping or the MPS allows Marine Corps forces to operate from a mobile seabase far from the enemy's shore. Seabasing allows the Marine Corps to bring ashore only those forces and assets essential to the mission. This provides the JFC with increased operational freedom, precluding the need to establish, man, and protect extensive shore-based facilities. The ability to conduct logistics and sustainment activities from the seabase, existing infrastructure ashore, or any combination will reduce the footprint ashore, thereby minimizing the threat to deployed forces.

Glossary

Section I. Acronyms

ACE ....aviation combat element

ACF.. air contingency force

ADCON ....administrative control

AF .... amphibious force

AO..area of operations

AT ....antiterrorism

ATF... amphibious task force

CAT .... crisis action team

CATF ....commander, amphibious task force

CE ....command element

CG2d MEB ....Commanding General,
2d Marine Expeditionary Brigade

CHOP.. change of operational control

CLF .... commander, landing force

COA ....course of action

COMMARFORLANT..........Commander, Marine Corps Forces, Atlantic

COMMARFORPAC...............Commander, Marine Corps Forces, Pacific

COMMARFORRES ....Commander, Marine Corps Forces Reserve

CONUS.. continental United States

CPG 2	Commander, Amphibious Group TWO
CSSE	combat service support element
CTF 62.1	Combined Task Force 62.1
FAST	Fleet Antiterrorism Security Team
FSCL	fire support coordination line
FSCM	fire support coordinating measure
GCE	ground combat element
HIDACZ	high-density airspace control zone
JFACC	joint force air component commander
JFC	joint force commander
JFLCC	joint force land component commander
JFMCC	joint force maritime component commander
JP	joint publication
LF	landing force
MAGTF	Marine air-ground task force
MARFORLANT	Marine Corps Forces, Atlantic
MARFORPAC	Marine Corps Forces, Pacific
MARFORRES	Marine Corps Forces Reserve
MCDP	Marine Corps doctrinal publication
MCRP	Marine Corps reference publication
MCWP	Marine Corps warfighting publication
MEB	Marine expeditionary brigade
MEB(AT)	Marine expeditionary brigade (antiterrorism)

MEF .... Marine expeditionary force

METT-T .... mission, enemy, terrain and weather,
troops and support available—time available

MEU.. Marine expeditionary unit

MEU(SOC) ....Marine expeditionary unit (special operations capable)

MOOTW .... military operations other than war

MPF .... maritime prepositioning force

MPS .... maritime prepositioning ships

MPSRON ....maritime prepositioning ships squadron

MSE ....major subordinate element

MTW .... major theater war

OMFTS ....operational maneuver from the sea

OPCON .... operational control

OPLAN .... operation plan

OPORD ....operation order

PHIBRON .... amphibious squadron

R2P2................................ rapid response planning process

STOM .... ship-to-objective maneuver

TACON... tactical control

TRAP .... tactical recovery of aircraft and personnel

UNAAF...................................... Unified Action Armed Forces

US ....United States

USSOCOM ....United States Special Operations Command

Section II. Definitions

action phase—In an amphibious operation, the period of time between the arrival of the landing forces of the amphibious force in the operational area and the accomplishment of their mission. See also **amphibious force; amphibious operation; landing force; mission.** (JP 1-02)

administrative control—Direction or exercise of authority over subordinate or other organizations in respect to administration and support, including organization of Service forces, control of resources and equipment, personnel management, unit logistics, individual and unit training, readiness, mobilization, demobilization, discipline, and other matters not included in the operational missions of the subordinate or other organizations. Also called **ADCON.** (JP 1-02)

air contingency MAGTF—An on-call, combat-ready MAGTF that deploys by airlift. Air contingency MAGTFs vary in size based on mission requirements and the availability of airlift. Because they deploy by air, they generally have a limited organic logistics capability, and require an arrival airfield. Air contingency MAGTFs usually are activated to respond to developing crises, and may deploy independently or in conjunction with other expeditionary forces. Also called **ACM.** See also **Marine air-ground task force; Marine expeditionary force; Marine expeditionary unit; special purpose Marine air-ground task force.** (Proposed for inclusion in MCRP 5-12C.)

airspace control order—An order implementing the airspace control plan that provides the details of the approved requests for airspace control measures. It is published either as part of the air tasking order or as a separate document. Also called **ACO.** (JP 1-02)

airspace control plan—The document approved by the joint force commander that provides specific planning guidance and procedures for the airspace control system for the joint force area of responsibility and/or joint operations area. Also called **ACP**. See also **area of responsibility**; **joint force commander**; **joint operations area**. (JP 1-02)

alliance—An alliance is the result of formal agreements (i.e., treaties) between two or more nations for broad, long-term objectives that further the common interests of the members. See also **coalition**; **multinational**. (JP 1-02)

amphibious force—An amphibious task force and a landing force together with other forces that are trained, organized, and equipped for amphibious operations. Also called **AF**. See also **amphibious operation**; **amphibious task force**; **landing force**. (JP 1-02)

amphibious objective area—A geographical area (delineated for command and control purposes in the order initiating the amphibious operation) within which is located the objective(s) to be secured by the amphibious force. This area must be of sufficient size to ensure accomplishment of the amphibious force's mission and must provide sufficient area for conducting necessary sea, air, and land operations. Also called **AOA**. See also **amphibious force**; **mission**.(JP 1-02)

amphibious operation—A military operation launched from the sea by an amphibious force, embarked in ships or craft with the primary purpose of introducing a landing force ashore to accomplish the assigned mission. See also **amphibious force**; **landing force**; **mission**. (JP 1-02)

amphibious task force—A Navy task organization formed to conduct amphibious operations. The amphibious task force, together with the landing force and other forces, constitutes the amphibious force. Also called **ATF**. See also **amphibious force**; **amphibious operation**; **landing force**. (JP 1-02)

area air defense commander—Within a unified command, subordinate unified command, or joint task force, the commander will assign overall responsibility for air defense to a single commander. Normally, this will be the component commander with the preponderance of air defense capability and the command, control, and communications capability to plan and execute integrated air defense operations. Representation from the other components involved will be provided, as appropriate, to the area defense commander's headquarters. Also called **AADC**. (JP 1-02)

area of influence—A geographical area wherein a commander is directly capable of influencing operations by maneuver or fire support systems normally under the commander's command or control. (JP 1-02)

area of interest—That area of concern to the commander, including the area of influence, areas adjacent thereto, and extending into enemy territory to the objectives of current or planned operations. This area also includes areas occupied by enemy forces who could jeopardize the accomplishment of the mission. Also called **AOI**. See also **area of influence**. (JP 1-02)

area of operations—An operational area defined by the joint force commander for land and naval forces. Areas of operation do not typically encompass the entire operational area of the joint force commander, but should be large enough for component commanders to accomplish their missions and protect their forces. Also called **AO**. See also **area of responsibility; joint operations area; joint special operations area**. (JP 1-02)

area of responsibility—The geographical area associated with a combatant command within which a combatant commander has authority to plan and conduct operations. Also called **AOR**. (JP 1-02)

battlespace—The environment, factors, and conditions that must be understood to successfully apply combat power, protect the force, or complete the mission. This includes the air, land, sea, space, and the included enemy and friendly forces; facilities; weather; terrain; the electromagnetic spectrum; and the information environment within the operational areas and areas of interest. (JP 1-02)

branch(es)—A contingency plan or course of action (an option built into the basic plan or course of action) for changing the mission, disposition, orientation, or direction of movement of the force to aid success of the operation based on anticipated events, opportunities, or disruptions caused by enemy actions. See also **sequel.** (MCRP 5-12C)

campaign—A series of related military operations aimed at accomplishing a strategic or operational objective within a given time and space. **NOTE: There is only one campaign, and it belongs to the joint commander.**

centers of gravity—Those characteristics, capabilities, or sources of power from which a military force derives its freedom of action, physical strength, or will to fight. Also called **COGs.** (JP 1-02)

change of operational control—The date and time (Coordinated Universal Time) at which a force or unit is reassigned or attached from one commander to another where the gaining commander will exercise operational control over that force or unit. Also called **CHOP.** See also **operational control.** (JP 1-02)

close air support—Air action by fixed- and rotary-wing aircraft against hostile targets that are in close proximity to friendly forces and that require detailed integration of each air mission with the fire and movement of those forces. Also called **CAS.** (JP 1-02)

coalition—An ad hoc arrangement between two or more nations for common action. See also **alliance; multinational.** (JP 1-02)

combatant command (command authority)—Nontransferable command authority established by title 10 ("Armed Forces"), United States Code, section 164, exercised only by commanders of unified or specified combatant commands unless otherwise directed by the President or the Secretary of Defense. Combatant command (command authority) cannot be delegated and is the authority of a combatant commander to perform those functions of command over assigned forces involving organizing and employing commands and forces, assigning tasks, designating objectives, and giving authoritative direction over all aspects of military operations, joint training, and logistics necessary to accomplish the missions assigned to the command. Combatant command (command authority) should be exercised through the commanders of subordinate organizations. Normally this authority is exercised through subordinate joint force commanders and Service and/or functional component commanders. Combatant command (command authority) provides full authority to organize and employ commands and forces as the combatant commander considers necessary to accomplish assigned missions. Operational control is inherent in combatant command (command authority). Also called **COCOM**. See also **combatant commander; operational control; tactical control.** (JP 1-02)

combatant commander—A commander of one of the unified or specified combatant commands established by the President. (JP 1-02)

combined arms—The full integration of combat arms in such a way that to counteract one, the enemy must become more vulnerable to another. (MCRP 5-12C)

command and control—The exercise of authority and direction by a properly designated commander over assigned and attached forces in the accomplishment of the mission. Command and control functions are performed through an arrangement of personnel, equipment, communications, facilities, and procedures employed by a commander in planning, directing, coordinating, and controlling forces and operations in the accomplishment of the mission. (JP 1-02) Also in Marine Corps usage, the means by which a commander recognizes what needs to be done and sees to it that appropriate actions are taken. Also called **C2**. (MCRP 5-12C)

commander, amphibious task force—The Navy officer designated in the order initiating the amphibious operation as the commander of the amphibious task force. Also called **CATF**. See also **amphibious operation; amphibious task force; commander, landing force.** (JP 1-02)

commander, landing force—The officer designated in the order initiating the amphibious operation as the commander of the landing force for an amphibious operation. Also called **CLF**. See also **amphibious operation; commander, amphibious task force; landing force.** (JP 1-02)

commander's intent—A commander's clear, concise articulation of the purpose(s) behind one or more tasks assigned to a subordinate. It is one of two parts of every mission statement which guides the exercise of initiative in the absence of instructions. (MCRP 5-12C)

commander's planning guidance—Directions and/or instructions which focus the staff's course of action development during the planning process. Also called **CPG**. (MCRP 5-12C)

command relationships—The interrelated responsibilities between commanders, as well as the operational authority exercised by commanders in the chain of command; defined further as combatant command (command authority), operational control, tactical control, or support. See also **combatant command (command authority); operational control; tactical control.** (JP 0-2)

component—1. One of the subordinate organizations that constitute a joint force. Normally a joint force is organized with a combination of Service and functional components. 2. In logistics, a part or combination of parts having a specific function, which can be installed or replaced only as an entity. Also called **COMP**. See also **functional component command**; **Service component command**. (JP 1-02)

course of action—1. Any sequence of activities that an individual or unit may follow. 2. A possible plan open to an individual or commander that would accomplish, or is related to the accomplishment of the mission. 3. The scheme adopted to accomplish a job or mission. 4. A line of conduct in an engagement. 5. A product of the Joint Operation Planning and Execution System concept development phase. Also called **COA**. (JP 1-02)

critical vulnerability—An aspect of a center of gravity that if exploited will do the most significant damage to an adversary's ability to resist. A vulnerability cannot be critical unless it undermines a key strength. Also called **CV**. (MCRP 5-12C)

deep operations—Military actions conducted against enemy capabilities which pose a potential threat to friendly forces. These military actions are designed to isolate, shape, and dominate the battlespace and influence future operations. (MCRP 5-12C)

defense in depth—The siting of mutually supporting defense positions designed to absorb and progressively weaken attack, prevent initial observations of the whole position by the enemy, and to allow the commander to maneuver the reserve. (JP 1-02)

embarkation phase—In amphibious operations, the phase that encompasses the orderly assembly of personnel and materiel and their subsequent loading aboard ships and/or aircraft in a sequence designed to meet the requirements of the landing force concept of operations ashore. (JP 1-02)

end state—The set of required conditions that defines achievement of the commander's objectives. (JP 1-02)

expeditionary force—An armed force organized to accomplish a specific objective in a foreign country. (JP 1-02)

fire support coordination line—A fire support coordinating measure that is established and adjusted by appropriate land or amphibious force commanders within their boundaries in consultation with superior, subordinate, supporting, and affected commanders. Fire support coordination lines (FSCLs) facilitate the expeditious attack of surface targets of opportunity beyond the coordinating measure. An FSCL does not divide an area of operations by defining a boundary between close and deep operations or a zone for close air support. The FSCL applies to all fires of air, land, and sea-based weapons systems using any type of ammunition. Forces attacking targets beyond an FSCL must inform all affected commanders in sufficient time to allow necessary reaction to avoid fratricide. Supporting elements attacking targets beyond the FSCL must ensure that the attack will not produce adverse attacks on, or to the rear of, the line. Short of an FSCL, all air-to-ground and surface-to-surface attack operations are controlled by the appropriate land or amphibious force commander. The FSCL should follow well-defined terrain features. Coordination of attacks beyond the FSCL is especially critical to commanders of air, land, and special operations forces. In exceptional circumstances, the inability to conduct this coordination will not preclude the attack of targets beyond the FSCL. However, failure to do so may increase the risk of fratricide and could waste limited resources. Also called **FSCL**. (JP 1-02)

Fleet Marine Force—A balanced force of combined arms comprising land, air, and service elements of the US Marine Corps. A Fleet Marine Force is an integral part of a US fleet and has the status of a type command. Also called **FMF**. (JP 1-02)

force protection—Actions taken to prevent or mitigate hostile actions against Department of Defense personnel (to include family members), resources, facilities, and critical information. These actions conserve the force's fighting potential so it can be applied at the decisive time and place and incorporate the coordinated and synchronized offensive and defensive measures to enable the effective employment of the joint force while degrading opportunities for the enemy. Force protection does not include actions to defeat the enemy or protect against accidents, weather, or disease. Also called **FP**. (JP 1-02)

force service support group—The combat service support element of the Marine expeditionary force (MEF). It is a permanently organized Fleet Marine Force command charged with providing combat service support beyond the organic capabilities of supported units of the MEF. If supporting a force of greater size, additional assets are necessary to augment its capabilities. Although permanently structured with eight functional battalions, task organizations from those battalions would normally support MEF operations over a wide geographic area. Also called **FSSG**. (MCRP 5-12C)

foreign humanitarian assistance—Programs conducted to relieve or reduce the results of natural or manmade disasters or other endemic conditions such as human pain, disease, hunger, or privation that might present a serious threat to life or that can result in great damage to or loss of property. Foreign humanitarian assistance (FHA) provided by US forces is limited in scope and duration. The foreign assistance provided is designed to supplement or complement the efforts of the host nation civil authorities or agencies that may have the primary responsibility for providing FHA. FHA operations are those conducted outside the United States, its territories, and possessions. Also called **FHA**. (JP 1-02)

forward deployment—A basic undertaking which entails stationing of alert forces with their basic stocks for extended periods of time at either land-based overseas facilities or, in maritime operations, aboard ships at sea as a means of enhancing national contingency response capabilities. (MCRP 5-12C)

forward edge of the battle area—The foremost limits of a series of areas in which ground combat units are deployed, excluding the areas in which the covering or screening forces are operating, designated to coordinate fire support, the positioning of forces, or the maneuver of units. Also called **FEBA**. (JP 1-02)

functional component command—A command normally, but not necessarily, composed of forces of two or more Military Departments which may be established across the range of military operations to perform particular operational missions that may be of short duration or may extend over a period of time. (JP 1-02)

H-hour (amphibious operations)—For amphibious operations, the time the first assault elements are scheduled to touch down on the beach, or a landing zone, and in some cases the commencement of countermine breaching operations. (JP 1-02)

high-density airspace control zone—Airspace designated in an airspace control plan or airspace control order, in which there is a concentrated employment of numerous and varied weapons and airspace users. A high-density airspace control zone has defined dimensions which usually coincide with geographical features or navigational aids. Access to a high-density airspace control zone is normally controlled by the maneuver commander. The maneuver commander can also direct a more restrictive weapons status within the high-density airspace control zone. Also called **HIDACZ**. (JP 1-02)

joint—Connotes activities, operations, organizations, etc., in which elements of two or more Military Departments participate. (JP 1-02)

joint amphibious operation—An amphibious operation conducted by significant elements of two or more Services.

joint force—A general term applied to a force composed of significant elements, assigned or attached, of two or more Military Departments operating under a single joint force commander. See also **joint force commander**. (JP 1-02)

joint force air component commander—The commander within a unified command, subordinate unified command, or joint task force responsible to the establishing commander for making recommendations on the proper employment of assigned, attached, and/or made available for tasking air forces; planning and coordinating air operations; or accomplishing such operational missions as may be assigned. The joint force air component commander is given the authority necessary to accomplish missions and tasks assigned by the establishing commander. Also called **JFACC**. See also **joint force commander**. (JP 1-02)

joint force commander—A general term applied to a combatant commander, subunified commander, or joint task force commander authorized to exercise combatant command (command authority) or operational control over a joint force. Also called **JFC**. See also **joint force**. (JP 1-02)

joint force land component commander—The commander within a unified command, subordinate unified command, or joint task force responsible to the establishing commander for making recommendations on the proper employment of assigned, attached, and/or made available for tasking land forces; planning and coordinating land operations; or accomplishing such operational missions as may be assigned. The joint force land component commander is given the authority necessary to accomplish missions and tasks assigned by the establishing commander. Also called **JFLCC**. See also **joint force commander**. (JP 1-02)

joint force maritime component commander—The commander within a unified command, subordinate unified command, or joint task force responsible to the establishing commander for making recommendations on the proper employment of assigned, attached, and/or made available for tasking maritime forces and assets; planning and coordinating maritime operations; or accomplishing such operational missions as may be assigned. The joint force maritime component commander is given the authority necessary to accomplish missions and tasks assigned by the establishing commander. Also called **JFMCC**. See also **joint force commander**. (JP 1-02)

joint force special operations component commander—The commander within a unified command, subordinate unified command, or joint task force responsible to the establishing commander for making recommendations on the proper employment of assigned, attached, and/or made available for tasking special operations forces and assets; planning and coordinating special operations; or accomplishing such operational missions as may be assigned. The joint force special operations component commander is given the authority necessary to accomplish missions and tasks assigned by the establishing commander. Also called **JFSOCC**. See also **joint force commander**. (JP 1-02)

joint operations—A general term to describe military actions conducted by joint forces or by Service forces in relationships (e.g., support, coordinating authority) which, of themselves, do not create joint forces. (JP 1-02)

joint operations area—An area of land, sea, and airspace, defined by a geographic combatant commander or subordinate unified commander, in which a joint force commander (normally a joint task force commander) conducts military operations to accomplish a specific mission. Joint operations areas are particularly useful when operations are limited in scope and geographic area or when operations are to be conducted on the boundaries between theaters. Also called **JOA**. See also **area of responsibility; joint special operations area**. (JP 1-02)

joint special operations area—A restricted area of land, sea, and airspace assigned by a joint force commander to the commander of a joint special operations force to conduct special operations activities. The commander of joint special operations forces may further assign a specific area or sector within the joint special operations area to a subordinate commander for mission execution. The scope and duration of the special operations forces' mission, friendly and hostile situation, and politico-military considerations all influence the number, composition, and sequencing of special operations forces deployed into a joint special operations area. It may be limited in size to accommodate a discrete direct action mission or may be extensive enough to allow a continuing broad range of unconventional warfare operations. Also called **JSOA**. (JP 1-02)

joint staff—1. The staff of a commander of a unified or specified command, subordinate unified command, joint task force, or subordinate functional component (when a functional component command will employ forces from more than one Military Department), that includes members from the several Services comprising the force. These members should be assigned in such a manner as to ensure that the commander understands the tactics, techniques, capabilities, needs, and limitations of the component parts of the force. Positions on the staff should be divided so that Service representation and influence generally reflect the Service composition of the force. 2. (capitalized as **Joint Staff**) The staff under the Chairman of the Joint Chiefs of Staff as provided for in the National Security Act of 1947, as amended by the Goldwater-Nichols Department of Defense Reorganization Act of 1986. The Joint Staff assists the Chairman and, subject to the authority, direction, and control of the Chairman and the other members of the Joint Chiefs of Staff in carrying out their responsibilities. Also called **JS**. (JP 1-02)

joint task force—A joint force that is constituted and so designated by the Secretary of Defense, a combatant commander, a subunified commander, or an existing joint task force commander. Also called **JTF**. (JP 1-02)

landing force—A Marine Corps or Army task organization formed to conduct amphibious operations. The landing force, together with the amphibious task force and other forces, constitute the amphibious force. Also called **LF**. See also **amphibious force; amphibious operation; amphibious task force; task organization.** (JP 1-02)

L-hour (amphibious operations)—In amphibious operations, the time at which the first helicopter of the helicopterborne assault wave touches down in the landing zone. (JP 1-02)

maneuver warfare—A warfighting philosophy that seeks to shatter the enemy's cohesion through a variety of rapid, focused, and unexpected actions which create a turbulent and rapidly deteriorating situation with which the enemy cannot cope. (MCRP 5-12C)

Marine aircraft wing—The Marine aircraft wing is the highest level aviation command in the Fleet Marine Force. The Marine aircraft wing is task-organized to provide a flexible and balanced air combat organization capable of providing the full range of combat air operations in a variety of areas without the requirement of prepositioned support, control, and logistic facilities. Only the wing has the inherent capability of performing all six aviation functions. Also called **MAW**. (MCRP 5-12C)

Marine air-ground task force—The Marine Corps principal organization for all missions across the range of military operations, composed of forces task-organized under a single commander capable of responding rapidly to a contingency anywhere in the world. The types of forces in the MAGTF are functionally grouped into four core elements: a command element, an aviation combat element, a ground combat element, and a combat service support element. The four core elements are categories of forces, not formal commands. The basic structure of the Marine air-ground task force never varies, though the number, size, and type of Marine Corps units comprising each of its four elements will always be mission dependent. The flexibility of the organizational structure allows for one or more subordinate MAGTFs to be assigned and other Service and/or foreign military forces to be assigned or attached to the MAGTF. Also called **MAGTF**. The four MAGTF elements are the—

command element—The core element of a Marine air-ground task force (MAGTF) that is the headquarters. The command element is composed of the commander, general or executive and special staff sections, headquarters section, and requisite communications support, intelligence and reconnaissance forces, necessary to accomplish the MAGTF's mission. The command element provides command and control, intelligence, and other support essential for effective planning and execution of operations by the other elements of the MAGTF. The command element varies in size and composition and may contain other Service or foreign military forces assigned or attached to the MAGTF. Also called **CE**.

aviation combat element—The core element of a Marine air-ground task force (MAGTF) that is task-organized to conduct aviation operations. The aviation combat element provides all or a portion of the six functions of Marine aviation necessary to accomplish the MAGTF's mission. These functions are antiair warfare, offensive air support, assault support, electronic warfare, air reconnaissance, and control of aircraft and missiles. The aviation combat element is usually composed of an aviation unit headquarters and various other aviation units or their detachments. It can vary in size from a small aviation detachment of specifically required aircraft to one or more Marine aircraft wings. The aviation combat element may contain other Service or foreign military forces assigned or attached to the MAGTF. The aviation combat element itself is not a formal command. Also called **ACE**.

ground combat element—The core element of a Marine air-ground task force (MAGTF) that is task-organized to conduct ground operations. It is usually constructed around an infantry organization but can vary in size from a small ground unit of any type, to one or more

Marine divisions that can be independently maneuvered under the direction of the MAGTF commander. It includes appropriate ground combat and combat support forces and may contain other Service or foreign military forces assigned or attached to the MAGTF. The ground combat element itself is not a formal command. Also called **GCE**.

combat service support element—The core element of a Marine air-ground task force that is task-organized to provide the combat service support necessary to accomplish the Marine air-ground task force mission. The combat service support element varies in size from a small detachment to one or more force service support groups. It provides supply, maintenance, transportation, general engineering, health services, and a variety of other services to the Marine air-ground task force. It may also contain other Service or foreign military forces assigned or attached to the MAGTF. The combat service support element itself is not a formal command. Also called **CSSE**.

See also **Marine expeditionary brigade; Marine expeditionary force; Marine expeditionary unit; special purpose Marine air-ground task force**. (Proposed for inclusion in MCRP 5-12C.)

Marine Corps Planning Process—A six-step methodology which helps organize the thought processes of the commander and staff throughout the planning and execution of military operations. It focuses on the threat and is based on the Marine Corps philosophy of maneuver warfare. It capitalizes on the principle of unity of command and supports the establishment and maintenance of tempo. The six steps consist of mission analysis, course of action development, course of action analysis, comparison/decision, orders development, and transition. Also called **MCPP**. **Note:** Tenets of the MCPP include top down planning, single battle concept, and integrated planning. (MCRP 5-12C)

Marine expeditionary brigade—A Marine air-ground task force that is constructed around a reinforced infantry regiment, a composite Marine aircraft group, and a brigade service support group. The Marine expeditionary brigade (MEB), commanded by a general officer, is task-organized to meet the requirements of a specific situation. It can function as part of a joint task force, or as the lead echelon of the Marine expeditionary force (MEF), or alone. It varies in size and composition, and is larger than a Marine expeditionary unit but smaller than a MEF. The MEB is capable of conducting missions across the full range of military operations. It may contain other Service or foreign military forces assigned or attached. Also called **MEB**. (Proposed for inclusion in MCRP 5-12C.)

Marine expeditionary force—The largest Marine air-ground task force and the Marine Corps principal warfighting organization, particularly for larger crises or contingencies. It is task-organized around a permanent command element and normally contains one or more Marine divisions, Marine aircraft wings, and Marine force service support groups. The Marine expeditionary force is capable of missions across the range of military operations, including amphibious assault and sustained operations ashore in any environment. It can operate from a sea base, a land base, or both. It may contain other Service or foreign military forces assigned or attached. Also called **MEF**. See also **Marine air-ground task force**; **Marine expeditionary brigade**; **Marine expeditionary unit**; **special purpose Marine air-ground task force**. (Proposed for inclusion in MCRP 5-12C.)

Marine expeditionary unit—A Marine air-ground task force that is constructed around an infantry battalion reinforced, a helicopter squadron reinforced, and a task-organized combat service support element. It normally fulfills Marine Corps forward seabased deployment requirements. The Marine expeditionary unit provides an immediate reaction capability for crisis response and is capable of limited combat operations. It may contain other Service or foreign military forces assigned or attached. Also called **MEU**. See also **Marine air-ground task force**;

Marine expeditionary brigade; Marine expeditionary force; Marine expeditionary unit (special operations capable); special purpose Marine air-ground task force. (Proposed for inclusion in MCRP 5-12C.)

Marine expeditionary unit (special operations capable)—The Marine Corps standard, forward-deployed, seabased expeditionary organization. The Marine expeditionary unit (special operations capable) MEU[SOC]) is a Marine expeditionary unit, augmented with selected personnel and equipment, that is trained and equipped with an enhanced capability to conduct amphibious operations and a variety of specialized missions, of limited scope and duration. These capabilities include specialized demolition, clandestine reconnaissance and surveillance, raids, in-extremis hostage recovery, and enabling operations for follow-on forces. The Marine expeditionary unit (special operations capable) is not a special operations force but, when directed by the President or Secretary or Defense, the combatant commander, and/or other operational commander, may conduct limited special operations in extremis, when other forces are inappropriate or unavailable. It may also contain other Service or foreign military forces assigned or attached to the Marine air-ground task force. Also called **MEU (SOC)**. See also **Marine air-ground task force; Marine expeditionary brigade; Marine expeditionary force; Marine expeditionary unit; special purpose Marine air-ground task force.** (Proposed for inclusion in MCRP 5-12C.)

maritime prepositioning force—A task organization of units under one commander formed for the purpose of introducing a MAGTF and its associated equipment and supplies into a secure area. The maritime prepositioning force is composed of a command element, a maritime prepositioning ships squadron, a MAGTF, and a Navy support element. Also called **MPF**. (MCRP 5-12C)

maritime prepositioning force operation—A rapid deployment and assembly of a Marine expeditionary force in a secure area using a combination of strategic airlift and forward-deployed maritime prepositioning ships. See also **Marine expeditionary force; maritime prepositioning ships.** (JP 1-02)

maritime prepositioning ships—Civilian-crewed, Military Sealift Command-chartered ships that are organized into three squadrons and are usually forward-deployed. These ships are loaded with prepositioned equipment and 30 days of supplies to support three Marine expeditionary brigades. Also called **MPS.** (JP 1-02)

maritime special purpose force—A task-organized force formed from elements of a Marine expeditionary unit (special operations capable) and naval special warfare forces that can be quickly tailored to a specific mission. The maritime special purpose force can execute on short notice a wide variety of missions in a supporting, supported, or unilateral role. It focuses on operations in a maritime environment and is capable of operations in conjunction with or in support of special operations forces. The maritime special purpose force is integral to and directly relies upon the Marine expeditionary unit (special operations capable) for all combat and combat service support. Also called **MSPF.** (JP 1-02)

marshalling area—1. The general area in which unit preparation areas and departure airfields may be located and from which air movement is initiated. 2. In amphibious operations, the designated area in which, as part of the mounting process, units are reorganized for embarkation; vehicles and equipment are prepared to move directly to embarkation areas; and housekeeping facilities are provided for troops by other units. (MCRP 5-12C)

military operations other than war—Operations that encompass the use of military capabilities across the range of military operations short of war. These military actions can be applied to complement any combination of the other instruments of national power and occur before, during, and after war. Also called **MOOTW**. (JP 1-02)

mission—1. The task, together with the purpose, that clearly indicates the action to be taken and the reason therefore. 2. In common usage, especially when applied to lower military units, a duty assigned to an individual or unit; a task. 3. The dispatching of one or more aircraft to accomplish one particular task. (JP 1-02)

mission statement—A short paragraph or sentence describing the task and purpose that clearly indicate the action to be taken and the reason therefore. It usually contains the elements of who, what, when, and where, and the reason therefore, but seldom specifies how. (MCRP 5-12A)

mission type order—1. Order issued to a lower unit that includes the accomplishment of the total mission assigned to the higher headquarters. 2. Order to a unit to perform a mission without specifying how it is to be accomplished. (JP 1-02)

movement phase—In amphibious operations, the period during which various elements of the amphibious force move from points of embarkation to the operational area. This move may be via rehearsal, staging, or rendezvous areas. The movement phase is completed when the various elements of the amphibious force arrive at their assigned positions in the operational area. See also **amphibious force; amphibious operation**. (JP 1-02)

multinational—Between two or more forces or agencies of two or more nations or coalition partners. See also **alliance; coalition**. (JP 1-02)

multinational force—A force composed of military elements of nations who have formed an alliance or coalition for some specific purpose. Also called **MNF**. See also **multinational operations**. (JP 1-02)

multinational operations—A collective term to describe military actions conducted by forces of two or more nations, usually undertaken within the structure of a coalition or alliance. See also **alliance; coalition**. (JP 1-02)

national military strategy—The art and science of distributing and applying military power to attain national objectives in peace and war. Also called **NMS**. (JP 1-02)

noncombatant evacuation operations—Operations directed by the Department of State, the Department of Defense, or other appropriate authority whereby noncombatants are evacuated from foreign countries when their lives are endangered by war, civil unrest, or natural disaster to safe havens or to the United States. Also called **NEO**. (JP 1-02)

operational area—An overarching term encompassing more descriptive terms for geographic areas in which military operations are conducted. Operational areas include, but are not limited to, such descriptors as area of responsibility, theater of war, theater of operations, joint operations area, amphibious objective area, joint special operations area, and area of operations. See also **amphibious objective area; area of operations; area of responsibility; joint operations area; joint special operations area; theater of operations**. (JP 1-02)

operational control—Command authority that may be exercised by commanders at any echelon at or below the level of combatant command. Operational control is inherent in combatant command (command authority) and may be delegated within the command. When forces are transferred between combatant commands, the command relationship the gaining commander will exercise (and the losing commander will relinquish) over these forces must be specified by the Secretary of Defense. Operational control is the authority to perform those functions of command over subordinate forces involving organizing and employing commands and forces, assigning tasks, designating objectives, and giving authoritative direction necessary to accomplish the mission. Operational control includes authoritative direction over all aspects of military operations and joint training necessary to accomplish missions assigned to the command. Operational control should be exercised through the commanders of subordinate organizations. Normally this authority is exercised through subordinate joint force commanders and Service and/or functional component commanders. Operational control normally provides full authority to organize commands and forces and to employ those forces as the commander in operational control considers necessary to accomplish assigned missions; it does not, in and of itself, include authoritative direction for logistics or matters of administration, discipline, internal organization, or unit training. Also called **OPCON**. See also **combatant command (command authority); tactical control.** (JP 1-02)

operational level of war—The level of war at which campaigns and major operations are planned, conducted, and sustained to accomplish strategic objectives within theaters or other operational areas. Activities at this level link tactics and strategy by establishing operational objectives needed to accomplish the strategic objectives, sequencing events to achieve the operational objectives, initiating actions, and applying resources to bring about and sustain these events. These activities imply a broader dimension of time or space than do tactics; they ensure the logistic and administrative support of tactical forces, and provide the means by which tactical successes are exploited to achieve strategic objectives. See also **strategic level of war; tactical level of war**. (JP 1-02)

operation order—A directive issued by a commander to subordinate commanders for the purpose of effecting the coordinated execution of an operation. Also called **OPORD**. (JP 1-02)

operation plan—Any plan, except for the Single Integrated Operational Plan, for the conduct of military operations. Plans are prepared by combatant commanders in response to requirements established by the Chairman of the Joint Chiefs of Staff and by commanders of subordinate commands in response to requirements tasked by the establishing unified commander. Operation plans are prepared in either a complete format (OPLAN) or as a concept plan (CONPLAN). The CONPLAN can be published with or without a time-phased force and deployment data (TPFDD) file. a. **OPLAN**—An operation plan for the conduct of joint operations that can be used as a basis for development of an operation order (OPORD). An OPLAN identifies the forces and supplies required to execute the combatant commander's Strategic Concept and a movement schedule of these resources to the theater of operations. The forces and supplies are identified in TPFDD files. OPLANs will include all phases of the tasked operation. The plan is prepared with the appropriate annexes, appendixes, and TPFDD files as described in the Joint Operation Planning and Execution System manuals containing planning policies, procedures, and formats. Also called **OPLAN**. b. **CONPLAN**—An operation plan in an abbreviated format that would require considerable expansion or alteration to convert it into an OPLAN or OPORD. A CONPLAN contains the combatant commander's Strategic Concept and those annexes and appendixes deemed necessary by the combatant commander to complete planning. Generally, detailed support requirements are not calculated and TPFDD files are not prepared. c. **CONPLAN with TPFDD**—A CONPLAN with TPFDD is the same as a CONPLAN except that it requires more detailed planning for phased deployment of forces. Also called **CONPLAN**. See also **operation order** .(JP 1-02)

peacekeeping—Military operations undertaken with the consent of all major parties to a dispute, designed to monitor and facilitate implementation of an agreement (ceasefire, truce, or other such agreement) and support diplomatic efforts to reach a long-term political settlement. (JP 1-02)

planning phase—In amphibious operations, the phase normally denoted by the period extending from the issuance of the order initiating the amphibious operation up to the embarkation phase. The planning phase may occur during movement or at any other time upon receipt of a new mission or change in the operational situation. See also **amphibious operation**. (JP 1-02)

power projection—The ability of a nation to apply all or some of its elements of national power—political, economic, informational, or military—to rapidly and effectively deploy and sustain forces in and from multiple dispersed locations to respond to crises, to contribute to deterrence, and to enhance regional stability. (JP 1-02)

reach back—The ability to exploit resources, capabilities, expertise, etc., not physically located in the theater or a joint operations area, when established. (MCRP 5-12C)

rehearsal phase—In amphibious operations, the period during which the prospective operation is practiced for the purpose of: (1) testing adequacy of plans, the timing of detailed operations, and the combat readiness of participating forces; (2) ensuring that all echelons are familiar with plans; and (3) testing communications-information systems. See also **amphibious operation**. (JP 1-02)

seabasing—In amphibious operations, a technique of basing certain landing force support functions aboard ship which decreases shore-based presence. See also **amphibious operation**. (JP 1-02)

security force—The detachment deployed between the main body and the enemy (to the front, flanks, or rear of the main body) tasked with the protection of the main body. The security force may be assigned a screening, guard, or covering mission. (MCRP 5-12C)

sequel—A major operation that follows the current major operation. Plans for a sequel are based on the possible outcomes (success, stalemate, or defeat) associated with the current operation. See also **branch**. (JP 1-02)

Service component command—A command consisting of the Service component commander and all those Service forces, such as individuals, units, detachments, organizations, and installations under that command, including the support forces that have been assigned to a combatant command or further assigned to a subordinate unified command or joint task force. See also **component; functional component command**. (JP 1-02)

special purpose Marine air-ground task force—A Marine air-ground task force organized, trained and equipped with narrowly focused capabilities. It is designed to accomplish a specific mission, often of limited scope and duration. It may be any size, but normally it is a relatively small force—the size of a Marine expeditionary unit or smaller. It may contain other Service or foreign military forces assigned or attached to the Marine air-ground task force. Also called **SPMAGTF**. See also **Marine air-ground task force; Marine expeditionary brigade; Marine expeditionary force; Marine expeditionary unit**. (Proposed for inclusion in MCRP 5-12C.)

staging area—1. **Amphibious or airborne**—A general locality between the mounting area and the objective of an amphibious or airborne expedition, through which the expedition or parts thereof pass after mounting, for refueling, regrouping of ships, and/or exercise, inspection, and redistribution of troops. (part 1 of a 2 part definition, JP 1-02)

strategic level of war—The level of war at which a nation, often as a member of a group of nations, determines national or multinational (alliance or coalition) security objectives and guidance, and develops and uses national resources to accomplish these objectives. Activities at this level establish national and multinational military objectives; sequence initiatives; define limits and assess risks for the use of military and other instruments of national power; develop global plans or theater war plans to achieve these objectives; and provide military forces and other capabilities in accordance with strategic plans. See also **operational level of war; tactical level of war.** (JP 1-02)

subordinate unified command—A command established by commanders of unified commands, when so authorized through the Chairman of the Joint Chiefs of Staff, to conduct operations on a continuing basis in accordance with the criteria set forth for unified commands. A subordinate unified command may be established on an area or functional basis. Commanders of subordinate unified commands have functions and responsibilities similar to those of the commanders of unified commands and exercise operational control of assigned commands and forces within the assigned operational area. Also called **subunified command.** See also **functional component command; operational control; unified command.** (JP 1-02)

supported commander—1. The commander having primary responsibility for all aspects of a task assigned by the Joint Strategic Capabilities Plan or other joint operation planning authority. In the context of joint operation planning, this term refers to the commander who prepares operation plans or operation orders in response to requirements of the Chairman of the Joint Chiefs of Staff. 2. In the context of a support command relationship, the commander who receives assistance from another commander's force or capabilities, and who is responsible for ensuring that the supporting commander understands the assistance required. See also **supporting commander.** (JP 1-02)

supporting arms—Weapons and weapons systems of all types employed to support forces by indirect or direct fire. (JP 1-02)

supporting commander—1. A commander who provides augmentation forces or other support to a supported commander or who develops a supporting plan. Includes the designated combatant commands and Defense agencies as appropriate. 2. In the context of a support command relationship, the commander who aids, protects, complements, or sustains another commanders force, and who is responsible for providing the assistance required by the supported commander. See also **supported commander**. (JP 1-02)

tactical control—Command authority over assigned or attached forces or commands, or military capability or forces made available for tasking, that is limited to the detailed direction and control of movements or maneuvers within the operational area necessary to accomplish missions or tasks assigned. Tactical control is inherent in operational control. Tactical control may be delegated to, and exercised at any level at or below the level of combatant command. When forces are transferred between combatant commands, the command relationship the gaining commander will exercise (and the losing commander will relinquish) over these forces must be specified by the Secretary of Defense. Tactical control provides sufficient authority for controlling and directing the application of force or tactical use of combat support assets within the assigned mission or task. Also called **TACON**. See also **combatant command (command authority); operational control**. (JP 1-02)

tactical level of war—The level of war at which battles and engagements are planned and executed to accomplish military objectives assigned to tactical units or task forces. Activities at this level focus on the ordered arrangement and maneuver of combat elements in relation to each other and to the enemy to achieve combat objectives. See also **operational level of war; strategic level of war**. (JP 1-02)

tactical recover of aircraft and personnel—A mission performed by an assigned and briefed aircrew for the specific purpose of the recovery of personnel, equipment, and/or aircraft when the tactical situation precludes search and rescue assets from responding and when survivors and their location have been confirmed. Also called **TRAP**. (MCRP 5-12C)

task organization—**1.** In the Navy, an organization which assigns to responsible commanders the means with which to accomplish their assigned tasks in any planned action. **2.** An organization table pertaining to a specific naval directive. (Joint Pub 1-02) In the Marine Corps, a temporary grouping of forces designed to accomplish a particular mission. Task organization involves the distribution of available assets to subordinate control headquarters by attachment or by placing assets in direct support or under the operational control of the subordinate. (MCRP 5-12C)

theater of operations—A subarea within a theater of war defined by the geographic combatant commander required to conduct or support specific combat operations. Different theaters of operations within the same theater of war will normally be geographically separate and focused on different enemy forces. Theaters of operations are usually of significant size, allowing for operations over extended periods of time. Also called **TO**. (JP 1-02)

unified action—A broad generic term that describes the wide scope of actions (including the synchronization of activities with governmental and nongovernmental agencies) taking place within unified commands, subordinate unified commands, or joint task forces under the overall direction of the commanders of those commands. See also **joint task force; subordinate unified command; unified command**. (JP 1-02)

Unified Action Armed Forces—A publication setting forth the policies, principles, doctrines, and functions governing the activities and performance of the Armed Forces of the United States when two or more Military Departments or Service elements thereof are acting together. Also called **UNAAF**. (JP 1-02)

unified command—A command with a broad continuing mission under a single commander and composed of significant assigned components of two or more Military Departments, that is established and so designated by the President through the Secretary of Defense with the advice and assistance of the Chairman of the Joint Chiefs of Staff. Also called **unified combatant command**. See also **combatant command (command authority); subordinate unified command.** (JP 1-02)

warfighting functions—The six mutually supporting military activities integrated in the conduct of all military operations are:
1. command and control—The means by which a commander recognizes what needs to be done and sees to it that appropriate actions are taken.
2. maneuver—The movement of forces for the purpose of gaining an advantage over the enemy.
3. fires—Those means used to delay, disrupt, degrade, or destroy enemy capabilities, forces, or facilities as well as affect the enemy's will to fight.
4. intelligence—Knowledge about the enemy or the surrounding environment needed to support decisionmaking.
5. logistics—All activities required to move and sustain military forces.
6. force protection—Actions or efforts used to safeguard own centers of gravity while protecting, concealing, reducing, or eliminating friendly critical vulnerabilities.
Also called **WF**. (MCRP 5-12C)

References

Department of Defense Directive 5100.1, *Functions of the Department of Defense and its Major Components*

Expeditionary Maneuver Warfare

Generic Intelligence Requirements Handbook

Goldwater-Nicols Department of Defense Reorganization Act of 1986

Joint Publication 0-2, *Unified Action Armed Forces (UNAAF)*

Joint Publication 1-02, *Department of Defense Dictionary of Military and Associated Terms*

Joint Publication 3-0, *Doctrine for Joint Operations*

Joint Publication 3-02, *Joint Doctrine for Amphibious Operations*

Marine Corps Doctrinal Publication 1-0, *Marine Corps Operations*

Marine Corps Doctrinal Publication 1-0.1, *Componency*

Marine Corps Doctrinal Publication 3, *Expeditionary Operations*

Marine Corps Doctrinal Publication 4, *Logistics*

Marine Corps Manual

Marine Corps Strategy 21

Marine Corps Warfighting Publication 3-40.7, *Joint Force Land Component Commander (JFLCC) Handbook*

Marine Corps Warfighting Publication 5-1, *Marine Corps Planning Process*

Title 10, United States Code: *Armed Forces*

www.ingramcontent.com/pod-product-compliance
Lightning Source LLC
Chambersburg PA
CBHW070927290526
45795CB00001B/449